T0287473

ERNIE!

Stephen Poxon

ERNIE!

Heartfelt Recollections of the
Footballing Legend Ernie Moss

First published by Pitch Publishing, 2023

Pitch Publishing
9 Donnington Park,
85 Birdham Road,
Chichester,
West Sussex,
PO20 7AJ
www.pitchpublishing.co.uk
info@pitchpublishing.co.uk

A CIP catalogue record is available for this book
from the British Library.

ISBN 978 1 80150 509 3

Typesetting and origination by Pitch Publishing
Printed and bound in Great Britain by TJ Books, Padstow

Contents

Foreword by Roy McFarland

'A very talented footballer who was also an outstanding gentleman'

IT IS my absolute pleasure to have been invited to contribute this foreword in memory of Ernie Moss, who was not only a colleague, but a friend too. In fact, I regard it as an honour to do so. When I was first approached with a request to make this contribution, I didn't need to hesitate for a moment, as I was happy to agree to it straight away.

I have had the privilege of meeting Jeff Astle's daughter, Dawn, and to observe some of her work in speaking up on behalf of retired footballers whose participation in the game we all love might be responsible for brain trauma and dementia in later life, a so-called 'industrial disease'. The importance of being a voice for those who have lost theirs, or are losing theirs, cannot be overestimated. Dawn's commitment to highlighting this issue merits our support, not least in memory of her beloved dad, an FA Cup Final hero of West Bromwich Albion in 1968 and a fine centre-forward who represented England five times, but of course out of respect for the hero of this particular book, Ernie Moss. Guys like those two (and many others) have given so much pleasure to thousands of fans over the years, season after season, that the game of football is indebted to them.

Now it's time for some of that debt to be repaid.

My sincere hope in endorsing these pages is that they will go at least some way towards improving medical research and to drawing attention to a dreadful illness that appears to be blighting the lives of so many former players and their loved ones.

Sadly, the newspapers seem to inform us of more such cases almost every day, and I think of giants of the sport such as the late, great Nobby Stiles, Dave Watson, and Gordon McQueen (to name just three of far too many) whose commitment to professional football has cost them dearly.

The plight of these well-known names, and of course the challenges faced by players upon whom the footballing spotlight might not have shone quite so brightly, but who are nevertheless every bit as entitled to our goodwill and help, is precisely why the Jeff Astle Foundation deserves all the backing it can find, with our best wishes.

It is also to be hoped that this book will prompt sympathetic and concerted practical action from both the Professional Footballers' Association and the Football Association, within whose power it lies to influence real change. Likewise, we need to see this campaign raised again and again in the national political arena. There is a great deal of work still to be done at such levels, but projects like this one represent important steps on a long road.

To that end, every purchase of *Ernie!* will result in a few more pounds and pennies being placed at the disposal of the foundation, providing much-needed funding. Thank you very much indeed for buying a copy. As a retired pro myself, you will know I speak from the heart. Please encourage your friends to buy their copies as well, bearing in mind all of the above.

I hope you enjoy these stories. I know I will.

As we look back and delve into happy and affectionate memories of Ernie Moss the footballer and Ernie Moss the man, we also look forward to a time when problems like the ones he faced are better understood and addressed.

My own personal recollections of Ernie are of a very talented footballer who was also an outstanding gentleman.

He and I both plied our trade in an era very different to the modern game, and it wouldn't be any sort of exaggeration to describe some of the matches from our time as players as nothing short of brutal! Plenty of skill was on offer, no doubt about it, but it was often mixed with a physical commitment that definitely sorted the men from the boys in no uncertain fashion.

It was by no means unusual for centre-forwards, for example, to deliberately and cunningly scrape their studs down the backs of a centre-half's legs whenever the referee wasn't looking, and plenty of other examples of such 'gamesmanship' were commonplace, Saturday after Saturday. For me, that was just part and parcel of a defender's lot, and you knew what to expect. There were some hard players on the scene, and nowadays, looking back, I am somewhat embarrassed to admit that I played my part in some of that no quarter asked, no quarter given style of football. No prisoners were taken, that's for sure!

The likes of Johnny Giles, Kenny Burns, Tommy Smith (dubbed 'The Anfield Iron' by his adoring, distinctly partisan fans on the Anfield Kop) and

Chelsea's Ron 'Chopper' Harris come to mind, alongside Norman 'Bites Yer Legs' Hunter and Joe Jordan, for example (those nicknames tell their own story!). They were all players who could undoubtedly play a fair bit, and whose playing ability is certainly not in question, but who, at the same time, definitely knew how to look after themselves in the rough and tumble of a bygone footballing age, the like of which we are unlikely ever to see again.

Ernie Moss, though, was a notable exception.

He was not only a gentleman off the field, but on it, too, which is all the more remarkable bearing in mind some of the stick he took as he toiled away up front; subtle kicks to his ankles, swift punches to his kidneys, sharp elbow jabs in the ribs, and whacks on the head. You name it, it was all dished out to Ernie over many years. I honestly believe, though, that it never even occurred to him to retaliate, or to play the game in that fashion. Ernie Moss was simply interested in scoring goals. He had no other agenda at all. He really was a lovely guy, a gentle soul, one of Chesterfield's own, and I can't imagine him ever having been nasty, not in a million years. What a credit to the game he was, and it is no surprise at all that he still carries legendary status within the annals of Football League history.

If memory serves correct, I once had the privilege of coming up against Ernie in a League Cup match, when Chesterfield had been drawn at home to my team, Derby County, so you can imagine the local rivalry at stake in what was a bit of a needle match, given that barely 30 miles separate those two places.

What sticks in my mind from that game, even now, all these years later, is the totally selfless attitude with which Ernie played. By which I mean that if he couldn't actually manage to put the ball in the net himself, he was always happy for a colleague to do so, which is not always the case for goal-hungry forwards eager to grab the limelight. Ernie really was the epitome of a professional who knew exactly what it meant to be a team player. In that sense, and with that unselfish attitude, he must have been a manager's dream, and a joy to play alongside.

Ernie's enduring popularity within Chesterfield Football Club hardly needs highlighting, but it speaks volumes for the high regard in which he was held that the club signed him on three separate occasions. They certainly wouldn't have paid good money to take him back if they didn't feel he had something to offer as a player but, crucially, also as an influential character off the field.

Granted, even by his own admission Ernie wasn't the most naturally gifted player ever to grace the game, and I don't think he ever really learned how to actually trap a ball! What he lacked in artistry, though, he more than made up for in dogged, authentic determination and effort. He would always, unfailingly, give you an honest 90 minutes, even if he wasn't playing particularly well one Saturday, for example. I don't think it ever crossed his mind to do anything but simply carry on challenging for every ball, in all weathers and in all circumstances, fully aware of his professional obligation to those who were paying his wages; the fans, that is, who had paid good money to see him play. He never let them down.

And, let's face it, no one becomes a professional club's record goalscorer without having something extra special about them, and neither does a man win as many promotions as Ernie Moss did during his playing days, unless they know their business. Star quality, that's what that is, and the unassuming Ernie had it in enormous quantities, hence the affection and respect in which he was held.

Ernie Moss: a gentleman, a hero, a friend, and a footballer who produced the goods season after season. I am absolutely delighted this book is being written in his honour.

A proud Liverpudlian, Roy McFarland enjoyed an illustrious playing career as one of the most highly respected players of his time. He played a total of 517 Football League games for Tranmere Rovers, Derby County and Bradford City, and represented England on 28 occasions before retiring to manage several clubs, including Derby and Chesterfield, gaining three promotions along the way. Famously, none other than Brian Clough and Peter Taylor signed McFarland for Derby when they were a Second Division side, a transfer commonly regarded as being pivotal in Derby's rise to become champions of England twice in the 1970s. In respect of services rendered to Derby both as a player and a manager, Roy was appointed to the board of directors in 2017, and at the time of writing he represents the club as an ambassador.

Introduction by Geoff Miller

'Ernie – a great friend'

WHEN A great mate and business partner sadly loses the opportunity to enjoy the richly deserved latter years of his life, due to a condition that renders him completely helpless, we naturally ponder the big questions: how? Why?

After many years of the friendliest association with Ernie, it was never more difficult for me to appreciate or comprehend his illness than on the day I knocked on the window of his front room, only to see him sitting, motionless, on the settee, Sudoku in hand, oblivious to anything else and with, apparently, no knowledge even of who I was. There was simply no response to my appearance at his window, or to my usual cheery greeting. Jenny, the love of Ernie's life, had gone out shopping, you see, and had, of necessity, locked the front door behind her in order to prevent Ernie leaving the house and in all likelihood, wandering away. This was all for his own safety and welfare, of course, and was an unfortunate necessity, and not by any means something Jenny ever really wanted to do, except for love of her husband.

Knocking once more in hopes of a chat, or at least Ernie's awareness that I had come to visit my old friend, I was waved away. This was, quite simply, heart-wrenching, and the man I saw was certainly not the Ernie Moss I had known and loved for a long time.

My personal (abridged) version of the Ernie Moss and Geoff Miller story is, for the purposes of this tribute book, only a relatively small account of a relationship which actually merits a much wider résumé. However, even with that limitation in mind, because there is simply so much I could say about Ernie, I am happy to share the following happy memories.

Having been selected by England to tour Australia in 1979, my fitness preparation necessitated gym work followed by a daily five-mile cross-country run. Towards the end of one of those runs, I happened to jog past the location where Chesterfield FC were training. The manager of the day, the highly respected Arthur Cox, stopped me and said he had seen me running on a few occasions, and asked if I would like to join 'the chaps' in their fitness routines, stating that group work was far more beneficial than individual training, and would therefore help me in my preparations.

Naturally, I readily accepted Arthur's kind offer and joined the partnership of Danny Wilson and Ernie Moss in group workouts. That was the start of my friendship with Ernie!

Ten years or so later, when age was taking its natural toll and our respective sporting careers were reaching what we referred to as their enforced termination, meaning that other options of earning a living were soon to be required, we were each, unbeknown to the other, looking to enter the sportswear retail business. Thankfully, a mutual friend of ours, who worked as an estate agent and might have been able to help us locate a suitable property, knew the situation and suggested we sit down over a beer to discuss a business partnership.

To cut the story short, the following year Moss & Miller Sports was formed. My great pal, Ian Botham, agreed to cut the tape for us on the opening day, so we were up and running, if you'll excuse the pun!

To be honest, the business never did bring great financial reward, but in one sense that paled into insignificance because we had some truly wonderful times together; moments spent reminiscing about sporting incidents, hours and hours of socialising, lively, friendly banter with the customers (which they absolutely loved), and every so often, a conversation about purchasing stock and so on.

The chats with some of our regular customers usually began with 'Ernie, talk us through those three sitters you missed last Saturday' or 'Geoff, I could have caught those two slip catches you dropped the other day, with my eyes closed'. Happy days indeed, which I will always remember with great fondness.

In such ways, working together and looking back on our time as professional sportsmen, our friendship simply grew and grew, based on good foundations of a love of sport, honesty, mutual respect, and humour.

Eventually, though, the day came for me to leave the shop in order to pursue another avenue of livelihood as an after-dinner speaker, a role I found surprisingly enjoyable. Requests for my services as a speaker began to multiply, which meant a straight and candid conversation with Ernie was called for, the upshot of which was that Ernie took over the reins of the shop as I moved on to pastures new.

Tragically, the first signs of Ernie's difficulties began to show themselves a few years later, when

Jenny started to notice subtle but telling changes in his business acumen and his general character. Sad to say, such signs were to become increasingly evident. Those abilities we had taken for granted in Ernie were, it seemed, beginning to fade and diminish, which was a painful spectacle.

Fast forwarding a little, the general consensus of opinion as to the likely root cause of Ernie's dilemma was that he was simply too good at heading a football. He had successfully plied his trade as a traditional target man centre-forward, which had of course necessitated years and years of relentless practice. Ernie was heading footballs day in and day out over the course of his long professional career; the consequences of which are now only too plain to see. Hour after hour spent at the training ground, and season after season of competitive games, were all beginning to take their toll on this fine individual.

I certainly think it is anything but coincidental that so many in the 'ball heading brigade' are now suffering as Ernie did. You hardly need me to remind you that we have lost some of our footballing heroes to this disease. I personally feel there is a very real need for the sporting and political authorities to do something about a situation that inflicts daily hardship on so many people. This is now a real necessity.

Part of the sadness is that Ernie Moss – everybody's friend, and certainly mine, and a pro who trained and played in a conscientious, dedicated manner – was unable to enjoy the fruits of his labour. That seems such a cruel irony. Had he perhaps not put quite so much effort into honing his skills, Ernie might have fared a little better. We'll never really know, of course, but playing or training half-heartedly was never Ernie's style anyway, which is precisely why, even now, mention of his name commands lasting respect.

I have never met anyone who has a bad word to say about Ernie, and that tells the whole story of the man. He really was a good bloke, a true professional, and a human being blessed with an honest heart and a great sense of humour.

I think one of the best 'Ernie lines' which summed up both our working relationship and our friendship cropped up during a discussion about a potential business outlay which would have undoubtedly tested our finances to the limit. Ernie, with characteristic humour and sensitivity, thought about the proposition for a little while, then said, 'Geoff, if I agreed with you, we would both be wrong!' What a great way of putting it and thereby defusing what might have been an awkward conversation. Typical Ernie!

Ernie Moss, my one-time training partner and business colleague, was above all else a great friend whose memory I will treasure.

Geoff Miller OBE, a native of Chesterfield, represented Derbyshire, Essex and England as a cricketer of some renown, playing in 34 Test matches and 25 one-day internationals. He played for Derbyshire from 1973 to 1986, captaining the side from 1979 to 1981. Geoff was an England selector from 2008 to 2013 and was appointed president of Derbyshire County Cricket Club in 2014. The cricket writer and journalist, Simon Hughes, referred to Miller as 'the only remaining player who unfailingly visited the opposing team's dressing room after play to thank them for the game ... [and] the last man to field at slip with a whoopee cushion up his jumper![1] *Miller was the Cricket Writers' Club Young Cricketer of the Year in 1976, and he was part of the Derbyshire side which won the National Westminster Bank Trophy. He ended the 1982 Boxing Day Test in Australia by catching out the legendary Aussie bowler Jeff Thomson.*

---

1   https://en.wikipedia.org/wiki/Geoff_Miller

Acknowledgements
by Stephen Poxon

MY OWN personal awareness of Ernie Moss was stirred sometime around 1992, when I had the privilege of studying alongside Mark Rose, who at that time was living in London, a very long way from his beloved Derbyshire. Mark's tribute to Ernie features elsewhere in these pages, but suffice it to say that he is an excellent ambassador for both his home county and Chesterfield Football Club, which he will talk about at the drop of a hat, with enthusiasm and what remains an abiding affection.

Back in the day, when we were both much younger men, Mark and I played for the same football team, and you didn't have to be with him long before you came to realise his game and playing style was largely based upon the admirable strengths and traits of his lifelong hero, Ernie Moss: total commitment, an honest performance, an excellent knack of playing to one's strengths, and a sheer unapologetic love of the game that never once dimmed, albeit Mark was a defender and Ernie was of course an out-and-out forward.

Ever since that time, and that initial introduction, I kept an eye on Ernie, coming to appreciate just what a giant of lower-league English football he really was, and, likewise, developing an understanding of just why he was (and still is) quite so revered as a local footballing hero and an outstanding human being.

Writing these pages, with so much invaluable, generous and heartfelt cooperation and help from Ernie's daughters, Sarah and Nikki, really has been a great privilege: a labour of love. It was such a desperately sad moment, though, when, with the manuscript almost finished, Sarah rang me at 6.23am one day to let me know that the final whistle on Ernie's life had sounded, quite suddenly and unexpectedly. That news came as a hammer blow, even though I had never had the honour of meeting Ernie personally, or ever seeing him play live, and I can only therefore try to imagine the truly devastating impact Ernie's somewhat abrupt departure had upon his family, whom he adored, and by whom he was loved beyond measure.

So, my very grateful thanks are extended to Mark Rose, and to Sarah and Nikki.

It goes without saying that my warmest sympathies and condolences are extended to the girls, to Jenny, Ernie's darling wife, and to the wider Moss family. They were privileged to know and love Ernie close-up, as it were, but they must now continue in the game of life with their star player having left the field of play. They will continue, of course, because they are made of strong northern stuff and because Ernie will have taught them how to do so, which is arguably his greatest legacy, but their grief remains personal, albeit somewhat in the spotlight. Ernie's example over many years will stand them in good stead, but I am certain I write on behalf of you all when I say we are, nevertheless, behind them all the way.

This book now carries an added poignancy in that it is written in Ernie's memory and becomes not only a tribute, but something of a keepsake too. That was never the original intention, and I shan't pretend it was, but the fact that Ernie passed away while I was still writing now lends something of a bittersweet beauty to the words of family, former players, friends and fans who have queued up to express their admiration. It is horribly sad that Ernie is no longer with us, and we wish he was still around, but this book will at least serve to honour his memory and comfort his loved ones.

I am, therefore, greatly indebted to everyone who has taken the time and trouble to send me stories, recollections and even the odd poem or two. The mix is rich and special, and it is worth noting the common denominator throughout; that every memory of Ernie quite patently came from the heart. I didn't once have to coax or persuade anyone at all to share their thoughts. In conversations, in emails, in texts and messages, that depth of sincerity has never been lacking. It will therefore be wonderful for the Moss family to know just how loved, respected and valued Ernie was, by some of the big names in the game and by 'ordinary' fans who admired him as one of their own.

I should perhaps add a courtesy note explaining that the contributions I have received are published here in no particular order, apart from those that refer to Ernie's funeral service, which have been kept together, for obvious reasons. I have deliberately mixed and mingled stories and recollections from players, managers and fans alike simply because I feel that's probably the way Ernie would have wanted it; football luminaries and former internationals, for example, paying tribute alongside people who have never made the headlines but whose interest in the game we all love is equally valid. I have a feeling Ernie would have approved, given that his own status in his chosen profession never once led him to entertain any notions that he was any more important than any other individual. The order in which these tributes appear is, therefore, a reflection of Ernie's basic ethos that this game belongs to us all, in equal measure. I hope you agree.

A mere 'thank you' seems barely adequate, but I can only hope each and every contributor knows and realises just how grateful I am. The honest truth is, without such contributions, there wouldn't even be a book. The goodwill and cooperation I have received while compiling these pages has been consistently impressive, and is deeply appreciated. My thanks go to one and all, famous and non-famous alike.

Thank you, too, to Michael South, whose support in terms of providing truly excellent photographs has been nothing less than invaluable. Michael has been supportive of this project throughout, and has willingly shared his photographic expertise, and his valuable time, with great generosity. Michael's input does of course stem from the fact that Ernie was his friend; everything else follows on from there, as is the case with so much of this content.

Michael's photography business is advertised elsewhere in the book, as a nod of appreciation for his cooperation, so please take a look at his advertisement and consider supporting his work by booking him and his camera for your special occasions.

A word of thanks also goes to Dawn Astle and Amanda Kopel, both of whom deserve all the credit there is for campaigning on behalf of footballers whose lives in retirement were blighted by dementia, quite possibly as a consequence of their devotion to professional football. Dawn's father, Jeff Astle, played with distinction for West Bromwich Albion and England, while Amanda's husband, Frank, most famously graced the colours of Dundee United. Dawn and Amanda have written bravely from a personal perspective, and I offer them both my wholehearted appreciation for having done so.

Jeff Astle and Frank Kopel battled dementia in their later years, and in honour of Ernie's similar struggle, I am delighted to say that ten per cent of any income this book generates will be donated to the Jeff Astle Foundation, while a further donation will be made to the Ernie Moss Memorial Campaign.

As a mark of respect to Ernie, I warmly encourage you to take some time to check out the footnote links that are included with Dawn's and Amanda's stories.

Those links are not only informative and interesting, but they also shine a light on what is an increasingly important topic of interest to fans and footballers alike. The more awareness there is, the better. Likewise, the link included with John Stiles's page in respect of his late father, England legend Nobby Stiles. Please have a look at them all.

I want to say thank you to Nick Johnson, head of media and communications at Chesterfield Football Club, and his colleagues, for their kind help and patience in negotiating various detailed aspects of publicity and marketing. Thanks, Nick. And, last but most definitely not least, a note of sincere appreciation to Jane Camillin at Pitch Publishing, for every encouragement along the way, and a lot of helpful advice.

Back cover photograph by Michael South.

The Jeff Astle Foundation

JEFF ASTLE was known for his outstanding footballing career at Notts County and West Bromwich Albion. Scorer of the winning goal in the 1968 FA Cup Final (one of only seven players in the history of the FA Cup to score in every round of the tournament), he was a member of Sir Alf Ramsey's 1970 World Cup squad.

Tragically, though, he will also be remembered as the first British professional footballer confirmed to have died from Chronic Traumatic Encephalopathy (CTE), a progressive, degenerative brain disease found in individuals (usually athletes) with a history of head injury, often as a result of multiple concussions. In Jeff's case, it was the low-level brain trauma believed to have been caused by the repeated heading of footballs.

Since Jeff's death in 2002, aged just 59, and despite the growing understanding of issues around head injury in sport and in particular CTE, awareness of these important topics still remains relatively low. The Jeff Astle Foundation was therefore launched in loving memory of Jeff as a fitting and lasting legacy that would raise awareness of brain injury in all forms of sport and to offer much-needed support to those similarly affected.

The foundation is always looking for partners to help achieve its goals. By partnering with the Jeff Astle Foundation, you can make a real difference to the lives of others. Their current partners support them in lots of different ways, ranging from personal funding to donations of items of sporting memorabilia for auction, for example. Please feel free to contact the foundation and find out more about becoming part of a winning team: http://www.thejeffastlefoundation.co.uk/become-a-partner.

The foundation's goals:

- The Jeff Astle Foundation exists to raise awareness of brain injury in sport at all levels, thereby providing education and support for current and future generations.
- The foundation will work with sports authorities and official bodies to develop guidelines on concussion and head injury in sport, from grassroots level to professional standard.

- One goal of the foundation is to nurture, support and deliver independent research into the links between brain injury in sport and degenerative brain disease, presenting findings and evidence to relevant sporting, medical and political bodies. The Jeff Astle Foundation will, for example, work closely with the Football Association and the Football Association's independent expert panel on concussion and head injury in sport, to promote research and action.

As well as campaigning in such ways, the foundation will endeavour to provide practical, emotional and financial support for sportspeople living with the effects of dementia or chronic neurological impairment; the ultimate goal being the establishment of a specialist care home for former sportspeople whose diagnosis means they require expert care and attention.

The foundation campaigns, lobbies, researches, fundraises, supports, and raises the profile of what is a growing area of concern, on behalf of those who are suffering, and their families, who are entitled to an adequate support system and financial assistance where necessary.

If you would like to know more about the work of the foundation, please feel free to get in touch. They would love to hear from you.

https://www.thejeffastlefoundation.co.uk/contact-us
dawnastle9@gmail.com

Warnock writes

Neil Warnock

'A genuine, honest player who always gave 100 per cent'

I was managing Scarborough at the time, and we were facing the prospect of relegation, so I spoke to my chairman and said, 'Let me sign Ernie Moss and we'll stay in the league.' Thankfully, the chairman sanctioned the deal, and Ernie arrived from Stockport County and played a massive part in helping us stay up. Truth to tell, he was probably past his playing best by then, but the impact he made on morale was worth its weight in gold – and points! I wanted to sign Ernie because of his experience and knowhow, and he didn't let me down.

I first encountered Ernie when he was a young lad, just starting out at Chesterfield in the 1960s; thin and gangly, but even then, a genuine, honest player who always gave 100 per cent. His game wasn't only about scoring goals, but about encouraging others too, which made a big difference both on and off the pitch. Ever since those early days in our respective careers, I regarded Ernie as a big, likeable lump!

I can honestly say I have never heard anyone say a bad word about Ernie, which is exceptional in the world of professional football. A lot of that was to do with his willingness to do anything for anyone, especially if it involved his beloved Chesterfield Football Club. He really loved that club, not just on the pitch, but as the special guest at countless numbers of presentations and awards evenings, that kind of thing. He would always give his time for the fans.

Ernie had a terrific sense of humour, which is a great asset to any manager, especially when the going gets tough and the dressing room needs a boost. I remember one evening when Scarborough were playing away to Torquay United and the late Steve Adams, another joker in our pack, was putting over cross after cross after cross. 'Addy' must have done that at least ten times, but Ernie just couldn't find the back of the net that night. I tore into the boys at half-time, reading them the riot act in no uncertain terms, after which Addy piped up, from the corner, 'I'm so sorry I've put all those pinpoint balls across, Ernie. I didn't mean to get you into trouble.'

Immediately, the tension was broken as the dressing room collapsed into laughter, at Ernie's expense. Typically, he took the joke in good sport, and we went on to win, 1-0.

It really concerns me, nowadays, to read reports of players like Ernie living with dementia, as he did, possibly as a consequence of repeatedly heading heavy balls. I was a winger, so I hardly ever headed the ball, but even so, it worries me how many stories might still emerge. It breaks my heart to think of that big, likeable lump having spent his final years in a nursing home.

Neil Warnock enjoyed a 'journeyman' playing career in the lower leagues of English football (being named player of the year at Hartlepool United in 1972), and has gained a reputation as a successful manager, leading unlikely teams to promotion time and time again. He is a popular figure among supporters who warm to his outspoken, down to earth style of management and his proven ability to turn around the fortunes of ailing clubs, often, to his credit, on a limited budget.

Three generations of Ernie fans

Gemma Davey

'The one and only legend, Ernie Moss!'

This is my memory of Ernie.

I first met the Moss family on Ernie Moss Day[2] at Chesterfield FC. I had always known about Ernie Moss, though, as my dad used to watch him play and always spoke very highly of him as a professional footballer. In fact, looking back, he was something of a household name. Growing up, I asked my dad lots of questions about Ernie as, sadly, I never actually knew Ernie the player myself.

Dad and I had attended the Ernie Moss Day to help contribute towards a charity fundraiser in support of people living with dementia. We particularly wanted to attend because we had lost my grandad (Dad's dad) to this cruel disease, back in 2012.

Never expecting a reply, but really just wanting to offer some goodwill and encouragement, I messaged Ernie's daughter, Nikki, after the event, to

---

2   In January 2015, Chesterfield declared their home match with Port Vale as Ernie Moss Day, when money was raised for dementia charities. This was so successful that it was repeated the following year, with all proceeds going to the Alzheimer's Society and Team Ernie, a fundraising group.

say congratulations, in the hope that they had raised a lot of money for a worthy cause. To my surprise, Nikki replied and the rest, as they say, is history.

In July 2016 I was getting married to Scott, and our wedding colours were those of Chesterfield Football Club, blue and white. At our reception, we wanted to name each table after a Chesterfield player, so I asked Nikki for permission to use Ernie's name. Typically, knowing the Moss family as I do now, permission was granted, and Nikki even asked Ernie to autograph some copies of the programme from Ernie Moss Day, to share among our guests. These went down a treat! It was a lovely, thoughtful gesture and definitely added a special touch to the day.

A few days after the wedding, Chesterfield were playing Matlock in a pre-season friendly, and I saw Nikki there with her husband, Stu, Nikki's mum, and Ernie. Noticing my sandals, he smiled, pointed to them and said 'shiny'. I have never forgotten this and never will. It made me smile then and still does now.

On the many subsequent occasions when I met Ernie, he never failed to make me smile, hold my hand or give me a hug. I will always treasure these memories.

So here's to the greatest player ever to grace a Chesterfield shirt – the one and only legend, Ernie Moss!

Gemma Davey is a lifelong supporter of Chesterfield and Swindon Town, having been born in Swindon. Her late grandfather was from Bolsover, as is her father. Gemma and her dad have been season ticket holders at Chesterfield for several years.

. . . .

John's jottings

John Farnsworth

'The lad's doing his best'

I was at a reserve match in 1984, and a chap called John Clayton was playing as a striker for Town[3] and missing quite a few chances.

A man sitting in front of me was giving the unfortunate Clayton some stick. Nothing unusual in that – a fan giving vent to his feelings! Happens all the time at any level of the game.

Unknown to me, though, Ernie Moss had come in and had sat down behind me in the near-empty stand.

The man in front (the heckler!) turned round, saw Ernie there, and began to complain about what a poor

---

3 'Town' is an affectionate nickname given by fans to Chesterfield FC.

player John Clayton was, probably expecting Ernie to agree with that analysis.

Straight away, Ernie spoke up in defence of a fellow footballer and said, 'The lad's doing his best. He's a good player, but he's just having some bad luck, that's all.'

As it happened, John Clayton left Chesterfield at the end of the season and signed for Tranmere Rovers, scoring 35 goals in his first season for them.

Just goes to show, Ernie wasn't such a bad judge of a decent forward!

John Farnsworth has watched Chesterfield play (first team and reserves alike) since he was an eight-year-old boy, in 1954. The first match he ever saw was an FA Cup tie against Hartlepool United, and he remembers Town losing 2-1 on that occasion.

. . . .

Chris comments

Chris 'Ged' Marples

'A true legend of my hometown football club'

Being a local lad, I recall my dad taking me to games at

Saltergate[4] in the 1969/70 season, when Chesterfield were crowned Fourth Division champions.

Wearing number eight that year was a young Ernie Moss, who had played with my dad at Chesterfield Tube Works. Little did I know that I would subsequently be part of the 1984/85 championship-winning team with Ernie still wearing that same number in the line-up! He was a truly amazing pro in his later years at Saltergate and I enjoyed my time with him in that memorable season.

Away from the games, I used to go to Ernie's sports shop, Moss & Miller, for football gloves, boots and so on, as well as getting my cricket equipment from Geoff Miller.

Our playing partnership continued when Ernie moved to Stockport County and I too was transferred there on deadline day. I regarded that as a privilege, as I commuted to Stockport daily with Ernie and Les Robinson, another former CFC trainee, meeting up at Moss & Miller for our daily journey.

As Stockport played their home games on Friday evenings, we travelled up to train in the mornings, then Colin Murphy, the manager, used to put us all

---

4   Saltergate (officially the Recreation Ground), was the home of Chesterfield Football Club from 1871 until the club's relocation to the Technique Stadium in 2010 (the Technique Stadium was formerly known as the b2net and the Proact).

up in a hotel for an afternoon nap. Ernie loved that, especially after our trip to the butty shop! Some of us younger lads used to go and put bets on, then watch the televised Friday horseracing.

It was a pleasure to play with Ernie at both Chesterfield and Stockport. He was a great example to the younger players of both clubs and even towards the end of his career he was always at the front of any training runs we did. After retiring I played alongside him in some testimonial matches and his enthusiasm was still there, undimmed.

Ernie Moss was always a man you could talk to, any time, anywhere. He is a true legend of my hometown football club, and in my opinion they should retire the number eight shirt in his honour. With respect to other Chesterfield players, no one will ever be as worthy of that shirt number as Ernie was.

Chris Marples has the unusual distinction of having played in the Football League as a goalkeeper, and as a wicketkeeper and batsman for Derbyshire County Cricket Club. His goalkeeping career ran from 1984 to 1995, beginning and ending with Chesterfield but also taking in spells with York City and Stockport County. He won a Fourth Division championship medal with Chesterfield and was part of the club's 1994/95 squad that won promotion from the fourth tier. Chris represented Derbyshire CCC in their second XI before graduating to first-class matches for the club as a first-team player.

. . . .

Joshua, journalism and jokes

Joshua Smith

'He was always a real pleasure to be around'

The first time I really met Ernie would have been around 2012. Me and my dad won tickets, as at the time the club was running a promotion whereby if you bought something from the club shop, your name was automatically entered into a raffle to win a hospitality matchday package, and me and my dad won! I can't remember who Chesterfield were playing that day, but it was Luis Boa Morte's first game for the club, so that would date it.

At half-time, as I'm sitting having a beer and my dad's at the bar getting a drink, who should come and sit next to me but the legend, and the very humble, Ernie Moss. He asked if the seat was taken, and I said, 'Not at all, and even if it was, you are more than welcome to it!' I'm sitting there in awe of this absolute club legend who has just sat down next to me!

We were watching Sky Sports News and he was pointing out all these different teams, and who they were and what they were like when he was playing. Teams like Barrow, and what a powerhouse they were in his day, and Halifax; talking about some of the battles he'd had with them, and Manchester City, saying that they weren't feared by anybody any more. It was just the most fascinating insight, not only into the man himself, but into football in general. To be looking at all these teams, it was almost topsy-turvy.

Those teams you would expect to be the minnows had been giants in their time. And Manchester City, who had always been a top-flight team in my lifetime, but were then in the Third Division. Ernie was telling me about goals he'd scored against different teams, and I just sat there, drinking it all in. Ernie was so humble. Then we shook hands and went back to watch the second half.

That memory has stayed with me ever since, and always will.

Another memory of Ernie arose because I worked closely with Jenny, Nikki, Sarah and all the family to help with the fundraising events and campaigns to which they were so tirelessly, endlessly, committed. I used my journalism training to help them, and I regard it as a privilege to have done so.

On one occasion, they had asked us to look after Ernie while they were at the bar, just to keep an eye on him really, and I noticed him deep in thought and conversation with my dad, the pair of them poring over the pages of a football programme and talking about the game.

Ernie's speech wasn't all that great at that time, to be honest, but the joy in his face, just talking about football, was special.

It brings a tear to my eye to remember two heroes in that moment, my dad and Ernie Moss, sitting chatting together, laughing and smiling. My dad has always been my hero, both of us season ticket holders going to Saltergate, much as Ernie has always been a hero to Sarah and Nikki, and Ernie was of course a legend. That was a really wonderful time.

And then as the years have gone on, whenever I've been with Ernie and his family, I remember those times when he loved to play the role of practical joker, poking me in the ear, for example, in the press box, when I was looking the other way, making me jump, or me giving Ernie a lift home in the car, with any number of distractions. All these things just epitomised who he was; that lovely sense of humour, joking. He never lost his fun side. He was always a real pleasure to be around.

Likewise, the love that I've seen surrounding Ernie over the years, especially with the journey towards his passing away, with his health declining. Doing the job I do, there is quite often sad news to cover and report, and the story of Ernie's passing was very sad, but at the same time quite beautiful, in the sense of all the tributes it inspired.

There was a great outpouring of love associated with that particular news.

My thoughts are with his family now. It's been a real privilege to have known Ernie Moss.

Joshua Smith is a father of two and a lifelong fan of Chesterfield FC. He has enjoyed a varied career in radio journalism since he graduated from the University of Derby. A successful sports writer and news presenter, he has broadcast on several radio stations in and around Derbyshire, and at the time of writing is the owner of Derbyshire Media Company (www. derbyshiremediacompany.co.uk). Joshua is heavily involved with presenting live radio and online commentaries of Chesterfield's games.

From miner to major

Mark Rose

'Ernie leapt like a gazelle'

At the age of seven I was finally deemed old enough to 'go t'watch t'Town wi' Grandad' and so the adventure began!

The excitement of the car journey from our home in Clowne, and the long walk from Grandad's favoured parking space near the railway station, up past the old hospital and along Saltergate to the ground, was indescribable!

The fear of my first-ever squeeze through the turnstile, and then the delight of sitting in the Wing Stand with Grandad and all his Saturday afternoon friends, was amazing. Sweets appeared from every pocket, with the strong smell of brandy as people opened their flasks of fortified coffee, and the whiff of pipe smoke, all adding to the experience.

The game began and that is where my memories of that day end; except, there was this one player who caught my imagination, and held it ever since. He worked, he ran, and he scored – a great headed goal that involved leaping high above surrounding defenders and directing the ball towards the far corner at the Cross Street end of the ground.

That was it, I was hooked! I fell in love with the Spireites[5] and that player in particular, who, as I was to discover, was Ernie Moss, or, as the crowd called him, 'Ernie! Ernie! Ernie!'

My admiration only ever grew as I saw many more of Ernie's goals over the years, including some special ones at Saltergate in memorable Anglo-Scottish Cup matches, and at Bramall Lane when Chesterfield beat Sheffield United on their own patch (Ernie hitting the bar with a header and the ball coming down on to the goalie's head and bouncing into the back of the net!).

Perhaps the greatest goal I ever saw Ernie score, though, was at Reading's Elm Park in the early 1980s. I was actually on holiday in Bognor Regis at the time, but me and some mates (one Sheffield Wednesday fan, one Sheffield United fan and one Barnsley fan) travelled up to watch Town on a Tuesday night.

As it happens, we lost the game, but that evening I saw Ernie at his impressive best. Ernie was being marked at a corner by Trevor Senior (who was no slouch) at the back post. The ball was swung in and

---

5   The nickname of Chesterfield FC.

Ernie leapt like a gazelle, towering above Senior to head the ball back across goal into the far corner.

Ernie was indeed my hero. He was during my childhood, and he remains so today, decades later, even though he is, sadly, no longer with us. If you doubt this, just ask anyone who knows me what my nickname is and they'll reply 'Ernie'. My first house was named 'Ernie's Patch' and my first pet was a rabbit named Ernie.

Need I go on! The fact is, I'm proud to bear his name as homage to all the joy he has brought to me over the years.

You may think it strange that a miner turned Salvation Army officer (Christian minister) would even have a hero, but that's the point: Ernie was no ordinary hero. He was never some fictitious character, and neither was his reputation built up by media hype. Ernie was a real-life, flesh-and-blood hero to thousands who saw him play.

Likewise, he was admired by those who managed him, or played alongside him, and by countless customers who chatted with him in his sports shop; essentially, those who understood his dedication to hard work and honest effort, not forgetting his trademark smile that simply said, 'I so enjoy scoring goals.'

Ernie's status as a hero is passed on from generation to generation of Town fans. Just ask my children – they know all about him!

It's been so difficult to see Ernie struggling with his illness, and as a person of faith, he and his family have been in my prayers. Hopefully our expressions of love for the big man have in some way helped his wife and children in these difficult days, especially since his sudden passing away.

We loved you, Ernie.

Major Mark Rose, a former coal miner, is a Salvation Army officer and a third-generation Chesterfield fan. A native of Clowne, he has seen his beloved Town play more times than he cares to remember, and wears the nickname Ernie with great pride, as a mark of respect and affection for Ernie Moss.

· · · ·

Captain's log

Russel Bromage

'You would always want him in your side, without question'

I was captain at Port Vale when 'Big Ern' turned up to play for us, and my recollection of him was that of a great professional, but not only that, a top man too.

Ernie Moss arrived at Vale with a reputation for being a dependable goalscorer in our level of football, and was well known within the game for being a good leader of the line, all of which proved to be true. His reputation was well deserved.

Ernie was in his late 30s when he came to us (though we used to joke he was actually in his late 40s!), which to be honest is pushing it a bit in pro football, but he had kept himself very fit and carried no weight at all. Travelling in with 'Newt' (Bob Newton) and 'Tarty' (Colin Tartt) on the so-called 'Chesterfield Express' train route, he still put in a decent shift and a hard day's running. Even as a senior player, Ernie could be relied upon as a forward. His attitude was the key, and in many ways summed him up.

I was a full-back and Ernie was great for us defenders because he always made himself available. He used to say, 'If you're struggling just hang it up and I will get there.' He was brave, always gave his all, and was a real nuisance to defenders, leading the line and putting the team first.

Throughout my years in football, I have been fortunate to play alongside a lot of decent forwards, but, with respect to everyone else, I would have to say that Big Ern was probably the best target man of them all. Granted, he was never blessed with lightning pace or a fantastic touch, but you would always want him in your side, without question.

Probably the best thing I can say about Ernie Moss was that he earned great respect not only from his team-mates, but also his opponents, the hallmark of a top man. When you start out in this game as a player, you want to have a long career, you want to achieve the best you can with the gifts you have been given, and you want to be respected by your colleagues. I think Ernie more than achieved all of those ambitions.

Oh, and I forgot to mention, a few of us liked cricket and Ernie was sometimes able to get Test match tickets for us, thanks to his friendship with his business partner, the Derbyshire and England cricketer Geoff Miller. What a bonus! Thanks, Ernie!

Russel Bromage played for Port Vale for a decade, from 1977 to 1987, and was their player of the year in 1981. He represented the Valiants on 402 occasions before moving on to play for several other clubs and then entering non-league football. Russel was twice chosen for the Professional Footballers' Association Team of the Year, in 1983 and again in 1985.

David's diary

David Slater

'Quite the local celebrity'

Ernie used to go to New Brimington Mount Tabor Sunday school as a boy, just round the corner from his Hollingwood home, just a decent goal kick away from Chesterfield itself.

Years later, in 1972, with Ernie by now quite the local celebrity, he was invited back to the church to distribute the Sunday school prizes. Unfortunately, though, he had suffered an injury on the Saturday prior to prize-giving and had to spend some time in hospital. Typical Ernie, though, he still made the effort to turn up on the Sunday (leg in pot!) in order to hand out prizes to 70 delighted children.

In my estimation, that commitment says a fair bit about Ernie, a man who never lost touch with his roots, and someone who could be relied upon to keep his word.

Incidentally, Ernie's near neighbours when he was a boy were two brothers, John and Roy Hickton, who both went on to become professional footballers, with Sheffield Wednesday and Chesterfield respectively. Quite a footballing neighbourhood!

David Slater had never been to a football match until he was aged 16, in 1955, when a pal took him to Saltergate. His early memories of standing behind the goal are quite vivid, especially remembering Ernie in action in the goalmouth. David says, 'Despite the sadness of Ernie's illness I do feel his rare talent has been recognised over the years. He will always be very special to me.'

New Brimington Mount Tabor Primitive Methodist Chapel, whose Sunday school Ernie Moss attended as a boy. (Photo credit: David Slater.)

Sproson says

Phil Sproson

'Meet you at the far post!'

Ernie Moss came to my club, Port Vale, late in his playing career, when I was about three years into mine.

We had a young side at the Vale, with many of us just beginning to make our way in the game, and Ernie's signing meant we really benefitted from his vast experience. I remember him always leading the front line well with his favourite quip, 'Meet you at the far post, Phil!' Ernie was a very powerful header of the ball, a skill I tried to emulate.

Ernie was part of our very successful promotion side in the 1982/83 season, and was always someone I looked up to, both on and off the field.

I recall going to the opening of his sports shop in Chesterfield. They were great days – happy times. I also saw Ernie at a Chesterfield v Port Vale fixture a couple of seasons back, when I was privileged to walk around the pitch at half-time, with Ernie and Bob Newton.

Towards the latter stages of his life, though, Ernie was far from well, a victim of the dreadful disease that so many former pro footballers dread. I send my very best wishes, and my love, to Ernie's family. They loved him, and he knew it.

A strong and technically competent defender, Phil Sproson played 500 games for Port Vale (426 in the league), placing him second in the all-time list of appearances for the club. The nephew of Port Vale defender Roy Sproson and son of Jess Sproson, who played for Vale between 1940 and 1947, Phil helped the Valiants to win promotion out of the Fourth Division in 1982/83 and 1985/86, and was twice named in the PFA Team of the Year. He subsequently played for Birmingham City until injury forced his retirement.

. . . .

Bright words

Mark Bright

'A consummate professional ... A wonderful human being'

The big man was a bit of a legend to me.

Ernie was a rugged, no-nonsense centre-forward who always gave 100 per cent in everything he did.

Career statistics of 850 games played (plus those that weren't recorded in official statistics), and 284 goals scored, speak for themselves. However, as impressive as those facts and figures are, I'd rather talk about Ernie Moss the man.

I was lucky because Ernie was at Port Vale during my first year as a professional footballer, in 1982, and I really couldn't have had a better mentor.

Ernie taught me how to be a good professional. He looked after himself, was a consummate professional, a good team-mate and more importantly, he was a wonderful human being.

As a seasoned pro, Ernie took time out to teach a young upstart how to play the coveted number nine role. In doing so, sharing the benefit of his vast experience, he was, ultimately, risking losing his own place, the better I became. He didn't resent it, though. Far from it. I think he saw it as his duty to help a young player starting out at the beginning of his career.

Ernie was always happy to selflessly pass on his knowledge, the things he'd learned over years of competing, so listening to him and working with him helped me enormously. So much so, I cannot express the gratitude I have for him for the time he spent with me; teaching, talking, encouraging, and generously showing me the ropes.

In those days at the Vale, press-ups and sit-ups at the end of every training session were the norm, and we were unfailingly encouraged by Ernie with his standard phrase, 'Oi! Come on, let's get them done!' That was the cue for players like me and Robbie Earle to drop down to the ground with Ernie, for sets of 25 press-ups and 25 sit-ups until we'd all completed 100 of each.

I feel very fortunate to have had someone like Ernie alongside me at that crucial early stage of my playing days.

There were of course plenty of other players who helped me too, I realise that, but none were more important than the 'Big Fella', Ernie Moss.

Staring out with Port Vale, Mark Bright is perhaps best remembered for playing for Crystal Palace and Sheffield Wednesday. In 1989 Mark won promotion out of the Second Division with Palace, going on to play in the 1990 FA Cup Final, and winning the Full Members' Cup in 1991. He was named in the PFA Second Division Team of the Year in 1987/88 and was Crystal Palace's player of the year in 1990. Moving to Sheffield Wednesday, Mark played in the 1993 League Cup Final and the 1993 FA Cup Final. His final achievement before retirement was helping Charlton Athletic win promotion to the Premier League in 1998.

Craig comments

Craig Hopkins

'I was very proud to have him as a friend'

I knew Ernie Moss for something like 30 years, and I have never had anything but love and respect for him and his family.

I've played alongside Ernie in charity games, for him as a player at Matlock Town, and I've sold sportswear to him as a sales rep. During my sales, I got into trouble for spending too much time in his shop, usually drinking tea and basically just having a craic!

I remember one occasion on which Ernie put a team together for a charity game, in support of a friend of mine who had been diagnosed with cancer. This was typical of him. Ernie was a great man; honest, warm and funny, in ways that weren't really anything to do with football but were just him as a person. I was always very proud to have him as a friend.

The story behind that gesture is that in 2005, one of my best mates discovered he had cancer and was facing the prospect of some very harsh and unpleasant treatment. He was patently seriously unwell and unable to work, resulting in the inevitable loss of income, and his problems were made even worse by the fact that he and his wife had two young children to look after and provide for.

Hoping to help my friend out financially, and to offer him some much needed moral support through traumatic days, I went to see Ernie with the idea of a charity fundraising game. He couldn't have been more helpful, 'Yep, no problem, just tell me where and when and I'll bring a team.' Just like that. No hesitation or reluctance.

Ernie was as good as his word, and the team he organised was full of ex-pros from Sheffield Wednesday, Sheffield United and Chesterfield. It was a great day and we raised a bigger sum of money than we had hoped for, which was of course really appreciated. For me, that episode just about summed Ernie up. He would do anything to help someone who was struggling.

Craig Hopkins started watching Chesterfield in the early 1980s, when he would sit in the same place at every home game, with his dad and his uncles, Stuart and Paul, in the Wing Stand, in line with the six-yard box. As a teenager he was a season ticket holder, and graduated to watching Chesterfield in some away fixtures too. He played non-league football for Shirebrook Colliery, King's Lynn, Kettering Town, Ilkeston Town, Hednesford,

Gresley Rovers and Matlock Town (which is where he was managed by Ernie), before going on to manage Heanor Town, Mickleover Sports and Matlock.

. . . .

Steve says

Steve Smith

'What a footballer, what a gentleman'

I have supported Chesterfield all my life and Ernie was a massive part of my introduction to the game. I saw Ernie play in his second and third spells with the club. For the last few seasons of Ernie's second spell, I was aged seven to ten, and every home game, without fail, Ernie used to come and say 'Hi!' to me and ruffle my hair when he came out for the warm-up, and sometimes after the match as well. He made me feel so special.

For several years after this, whenever I was playing football on The Green in Alfreton, while all my mates were pretending to be Zico, Platini, Maradona or Sócrates, I was always Moss! Everything Moss! I got ridiculed by some of my friends as most of them supported bigger clubs like Derby County, Nottingham Forest, Manchester United or Liverpool, and I was out on my own as a Chesterfield fan. It never bothered me, though. I was Moss and proud!

During Ernie's third spell at the club, when we won the Fourth Division championship in 1985, I remember playing on The Green (pretending to be Ernie, of course!), when my mate Kirby went in to get a drink and a biscuit, then came running out shouting 'Chesterfield have drawn at Peterborough!' This meant Chesterfield had been promoted and I set off on a lap of The Green. I went on to score eight goals as Ernie that afternoon!

After that title triumph, my proudest moment came when Ernie actually presented me with his shirt. To say I was elated is an understatement. Now, I really was Ernie on The Green, and I had the shirt to prove it!

Subsequently, I have been honoured to have been invited by Ernie's family to support Ernie Moss Day and to attend fundraising dinners, even getting to sit next to the great man. What a privilege!

It has also been a real privilege to know Ernie and his wonderful daughters Sarah and Nikki and of course Jenny, Ernie's lovely wife.

What a footballer, what a gentleman.

Steve Smith is a lifelong Spireites fan, from Alfreton.

Rudge remembers

John Rudge

'One of the nicest people I've ever met or worked with'

Thank you for inviting me to share a few words about Ernie Moss.

Ernie was a terrific footballer; player of the year for Port Vale in 1982, having joined just the year before and quickly establishing himself as a favourite with the fans. Quite a few of them still remember him as a fine player.

More than that, though, Ernie was a gentleman, one of the nicest people I've ever met or worked with, always willing to help others and to encourage the younger players with advice.

It's terribly sad to think of Ernie's heartbreaking struggle with dementia. I've been one of the lucky ones, working with Port Vale and Stoke City, but Ernie's situation is all too familiar these days, so I'm pleased to see it's under review. I hope this book helps to draw some attention to the problems, as it seems so many old pros are struggling.

Of course, the balls they use nowadays are nothing like the ones Ernie and I used when we were young players; great big heavy things, they were, especially when they were wet.

We used to have to train most days by running around a cinder or ash track that ran alongside the pitch, when footballs would be dangled above our heads on long poles that seemed to be about ten feet in the air. As we ran around the track, we had to jump and head the ball whenever we passed a pole. I reckon we must have headed those heavy balls at least 30 times every day.

Bearing all that in mind, I realise I've been one of the lucky ones.

John Rudge enjoyed a successful playing career as a forward for Huddersfield Town, Carlisle United, Torquay United, Bristol Rovers and Bournemouth, before going on to manage Port Vale for 16 years, the longest managerial spell in the club's history.

He led Vale to promotion in 1986, 1989 and 1994, to the final of the Anglo-Italian Cup in 1996, and to victory in the Football League Trophy Final of 1993. John also worked as director of football at Stoke City for a spell.

Frank talk

Amanda Kopel

*'I will never forget a wonderful photo of
Ernie Moss proudly wearing his Frank's
Law shirt'*

My late husband Frankie played for Manchester
United, Blackburn Rovers, Dundee United, and
Arbroath. He was also assistant manager at Forfar
Athletic.

Tragically, Frankie was diagnosed with dementia
the week before his 60th birthday, and lost his battle just
a matter of 19 days after his 65th. Chronic Traumatic
Encephalopathy was discovered as a result of brain
scans conducted by consultant neuropsychologist
Professor Willie Stewart, a deterioration likely to have
been cause by repeated head traumas.

That horrible diagnosis inevitably led to a
conclusion that Frank's career in professional football
had contributed to such traumas, and the irony of that
connection is nothing less than tragic.

This discovery, and my own personal research
into the subject, brought me into contact with
Ernie Moss and his family, and also with our
mutual friend, Dawn Astle. Thankfully, they all

combined to help me in my fight for justice as I sought to highlight the plight of footballers whose chosen profession had almost certainly caused neurological trauma.

To add insult to injury, so many of those players were (and still are) abandoned without much assistance or support. Dementia is no respecter of age, creed, colour or gender when it strikes. Just ask the Moss family, or the Astles, and other footballing families. It is surely no coincidence that so many men who played the beautiful game for a living, have been diagnosed with dementia in one form or another.

In memory of Frankie, I campaigned for Frank's Law, a campaign Frankie and I had launched in 2013 after discovering that in Scotland, anyone under the age of 65 was obliged to self-fund personal care if they had been successfully assessed for it, regardless of their illness or the severity of their plight. (Those over the age of 65 were exempt from any such charges.)[6]

Our campaigning challenged such unfair discrimination. Thankfully, we succeeded, and on 1 April 2019, after a six-year struggle, the Scottish

---

6   http://www.heraldscotland.com/mobile/news/home-news/
    footballers-widow-what-i-want-is-for-the-government-and-the-
    medical-profession-to-sit.117403661

Parliament implemented a law abolishing the discrepancy.[7]

It had been a colossal political fight, even though I realise it was nothing, relatively speaking, compared to Frankie's ordeal with dementia. Sadly, my beloved husband passed away as a consequence of the disease, but that is exactly why it is so important this issue remains firmly in the headlines.

Football fans everywhere, regardless of the team they individually support, owe it to the memory of their heroes to lobby for change. I personally owe it to Frank.

In order to publicise Frank's Law and to try to encourage vital media interest, we had T-shirts made (in tangerine and black, the colours of Frankie's beloved Dundee United), followed by some more printed in the colours of other teams Frankie had played for, all embossed with the Frank's Law logo.

I will never forget a wonderful photo of Ernie Moss proudly wearing his Frank's Law shirt!

Likewise, I was delighted that the Chesterfield squad autographed a T-shirt to be auctioned, along with other items carrying the signatures of sporting celebrities from all over the United Kingdom and

---

7   https://www.gov.scot/news/franks-law/

Europe, representing not only football, but cricket, golf and tennis too; an international sporting family. A memorable auction was held at a special Frank Kopel dinner held in his honour.[8]

Thanks to supporters such as the Moss family, funds were raised for a number of organisations involved in crucial research into this illness.[9]

My heart and soul went out to Ernie Moss and his loved ones as they watched Ernie live with the same affliction as Frankie. They, and other families like them, deserve all the help there is.

Amanda Kopel remains deeply grateful to those members of the Scottish Parliament who stood alongside her when she most needed their backing. A tireless campaigner on behalf of others in similar predicaments, she thoroughly deserves these pages in this book, and I warmly encourage you to read the information referred to in all the footnotes that accompany her words.[10] Quite rightly, Amanda Kopel was awarded the MBE in 2019, in recognition

8 https://www.thecourier.co.uk/fp/news/local/dundee/410351/frank-kopel-foundation-to-be-established-in-dundee-united-legends-memory/

9 https://www.arbroathfc.co.uk/franks-law-charity-dinner-and-auction/

10 https://www.sundaypost.com/fp/video-amanda-kopel-humbled-and-honoured-as-franks-law-campaigning-recognised-at-scotlands-dementia-awards/

of her efforts.[11] *Scott Kopel, Frank and Amanda's son,
enjoyed a brief career as a professional footballer, and was
also assistant manager at Montrose FC for a time.*

· · · ·

Tom tells his story …

Tom Bates

'A footballing legend'

Ernie Moss was nothing less than a footballing
legend, the local boy who made good; Chesterfield
Football Club's all-time leading goalscorer with 165
league goals, none of which, he always pointed out,
with the pride of a genuine striker, were penalties!

The year was 1966, and England had just won
the World Cup at Wembley when Ernie Moss left
school and took a job as a local government officer at
the Derbyshire County Council offices in Matlock.
Somewhat inevitably, he was soon playing for the
staff team and had early spells in local football
with Chesterfield Tube Works before playing for
Chesterfield Juniors and being invited to train
with Chesterfield's reserves. The manager at the

---

11 https://www.thecourier.co.uk/fp/news/scotland/793219/local-honours/

time, Jim McGuigan, was suitably impressed by the lanky goalscoring youngster and signed Ernie on professional terms at Saltergate in October 1968.

Ernie made his debut against Barnsley's reserves, and then scored in FA Cup ties against Skelmersdale and Wrexham before netting his first league goal for Chesterfield against Brentford.

The following season, Ernie won the first of his three championship winners' medals when he topped the goalscoring charts at Saltergate with 20 goals as the Blues won the old Fourth Division title and were promoted. All Blues fans over the age of 40 will remember his four goals at Saltergate that season, against Newport County! Vintage memories indeed.

In 1970 he had scored ten goals in the Third Division before the end of October, but then suffered a bad ankle injury when he ruptured ligaments in a fixture at Swansea and missed most of the rest of that season.

He met his wife-to-be at a cricket match, of all places! Jenny was a nurse, and they married at St Bartholomew's Church in Clay Cross, Chesterfield, on Boxing Day 1971. They have two daughters – Nikki, born in December 1974, and Sarah, who arrived in May 1977.

Ernie had a brief spell at Peterborough United and then joined Mansfield Town where he won the second of his championship medals by helping them into the old Second Division in 1977. He returned for his second spell with Chesterfield and won his third championship medal in the promotion-winning side of 1979/80.

He also played in promotion-winning sides at both Port Vale and Doncaster Rovers during a professional career which spanned over two decades and took in a host of other league clubs such as Lincoln City, Stockport County, Scarborough and Rochdale. Ernie made 744 league and FA Cup appearances, scoring a total of 245 league goals.

He played his last league game, for Rochdale against Newport County, when he was 38 years old, and then joined non-league Kettering Town, who he later rejoined after moving elsewhere and was 42 when he finished playing for them, a remarkable playing achievement by any standards.

He had spells in management at a number of non-league clubs, including Gainsborough Trinity, remaining as passionate and enthusiastic about his football throughout, and occasionally turning out in charity matches for Johnny Quinn's All Stars. Likewise, he was active in raising money for

Cancer Research and junior football development initiatives.

A true sporting ambassador, Ernie Moss was regarded as a model professional by his footballing colleagues and even now his name commands respect throughout the game, from fans and players alike.

Edited from a magazine article originally written by Tom Bates over 20 years ago. Tom comes from a footballing family, and found his own playing level in the Chesterfield Sunday League, Chesterfield Amateur League and Notts Alliance, from 1968 to 1986, with a variety of clubs. Tom became a committed Spireite when his uncle Ernie took him to a game at Saltergate in the 1956/57 season. He is a shareholder in Chesterfield Football Club, and helps to sponsor the club's academy. Tom has authored and published several books.

. . . .

Cratchley's comments

Ian Cratchley

'My genuine hero'

As a child growing up, Ernie Moss was my genuine hero, to the extent that in later life (in my wedding speech, actually), I likened Ernie's impact upon my childhood to the way in which another generation would remember David Beckham in his heyday. People tend to advise you against meeting your heroes, in case it's something of a disappointment, coming into contact with those you have only previously admired from afar. For me, though, when it came to Ernie Moss, quite the opposite was true, and it was great when he, his wife Jenny, and his daughters Nikki and Sarah, became close family friends. Imagine my delight, as a grown man, at having a garden kick-about with my boyhood idol!

I look at some of today's players and I am sure their managers sometimes wish they demonstrated even half of Ernie's wholehearted dedication. There was never a day when 'Ern' didn't fancy playing, and I think that's at least part of the reason he was always so popular as a player; highly regarded by colleagues and fans alike because he never gave less than 100 per cent. Supporters who have paid good money to watch games are entitled to expect that, and I don't think Ernie ever disappointed in that regard, at any stage of his long career.

Personally, I've always felt Ernie was underrated as a centre-forward, and never quite received the recognition he deserved. No one gets to play 850 senior games on the back of just working hard, and had he been playing today, there's no doubt he would have been much better rewarded than he was back then.

I used to love listening to Ernie reminisce about his on-pitch battles with Dave (Cyril) Cusack, or the time Sam Allardyce inflicted a broken cheekbone on him! He remembered playing against a young, up-and-coming Paul Gascoigne, in a Scarborough United v Newcastle United pre-season friendly once, when Gazza somehow managed to break the nose of one of the Scarborough lads. I was fortunate enough to play a few games alongside Ernie, and even when he retired from playing professionally, he remained fiercely competitive. He hated anyone giving the ball away and kept himself in great shape; it's not surprising, really, that he was renowned for leading the cross-country races in pre-season.

Socially, we never knew him have more than a shandy to drink, which no doubt accounted for his lasting fitness and the longevity of his playing career. Towards the end of his days as a player, we often took Ernie to games at Stockport County and Rochdale, when he was on loan, and again, without fail, we witnessed the same preparation for games that had stood him in such good stead, regardless of the level at which he was competing: fully focused and totally committed.

Ian Cratchley was 'born into a family of Spireites' and grew up following Chesterfield home and away with his dad and his brother. Ian's late father had at one stage visited 91 of the 92 Football League grounds and on one occasion, should have been going to China on business, but went to Northumberland for a Blyth Spartans v Chesterfield match instead, catching up with his colleagues four days later! David's father Ian was a member of the Ernie Moss Testimonial Committee. The Cratchley family greatly value their lasting friendship with the Moss family.

. . . .

Joking with Jarvis

Malcolm Jarvis

'Generous to a fault, and a gentleman'

My little story about our legend:

While I was playing for and generally helping to run a Chesterfield Sunday League team, I was involved in ordering our kit from Moss & Miller. On one occasion, having collected it and taken it home, I found we had only been given ten pairs of socks, so I went straight back to the shop.

I explained the problem to Ernie, and his deadpan reply was, 'Well, can't you just play with ten men on Sunday while I order more socks for you?' He said it in such a serious way, and without the trace of a smile on his face, that I thought he actually meant it and replied, 'No, we ****** can't!'

Ernie broke into a smile and said, 'I'm only joking!' Then he gave me a couple of pairs of socks that were similar to those I needed, while ordering me some more of the originals.

My old man absolutely idolised Ernie, not least because my dad worked as a volunteer for Samaritans, and Ernie often donated autographed items and memorabilia to help with fundraising for that charity.

Ernie Moss was generous to a fault, and a gentleman. I feel honoured to have hardly missed a game he played for Chesterfield.

Malcolm Jarvis is a Chesterfield fan through and through, and the sort of personality without whom lower-league, non-league and amateur football would be distinctly poorer. He represents the hundreds of supporters who give of their time, money and energy just out of a sheer love of the game.

Rob and Rialto Ceramix

Robert Lally

'Ernie held my hand'

It was in July 2017 that I received a call from Chesterfield 'superfan' Phil Tooley, commissioning me to construct a mosaic of Ernie Moss based on an image by Alan Roe, which is itself a family favourite.

I was already aware of Ernie's hero status within both Chesterfield the football club and Chesterfield the town, thanks to my previous connection with CFC when completing a mosaic of all-time appearances record holder Dave Blakey (I must admit, though, that I wasn't previously aware of any Chesterfield players as I'm from Salford, not Derbyshire).

The mosaic was finished a couple of days before deadline, so Phil and I fixed it to the wall in the club's reception area, ready for unveiling the next day, 19 August.

On the day itself, the scene was set for Ernie's family to unveil the piece, but they had no idea what was actually behind the cover. Whenever I have completed a piece of work that is special to someone, and has sentimental value, I am always nervous and apprehensive before they've seen my depiction of the subject matter for themselves. It's one thing for me to think I've succeeded in portraying a favourable image that people will like, but other people's opinions are much more important because of what my work means to them on a personal basis. What they think is more important than what I think!

The big moment came at 1.24pm (it's etched into my memory!), when my mosaic was unveiled, with the whole event being filmed for the UKTV channel. The sense of anticipation was palpable! Suffice to say, my nerves were jangling!

When the curtain was pulled back, I could hear gasps of amazement.

As joy turned to emotion, tears began to flow and the Moss family asked who had created this unique piece of artwork. I was then directed towards them and received a hug of gratitude from Sarah Moss with the words 'thank you' and 'it's amazing'. I knew then that I had completed a piece that was loved, which is always my aim when creating artwork for anybody. The apprehension! The shock! The joy! It's all there.

Ernie held my hand as photographs were taken and the conversation continued, and that act in itself meant the world to me!

Robert Lally is a highly talented ceramic artist specialising in distinctive mosaics featuring a varied range of subjects and people. Rob's excellent work can be viewed on his website, which includes a section devoted to Chesterfield Football Club: https://rialtoceramix.co.uk/.

. . . .

Support for Stiles

John Stiles

'A warm, kind, beautiful person'

I actually had the pleasure of playing for Ernie Moss at the end of my career at Gainsborough Trinity, and I immediately realised he had a deep knowledge of football, and an equally deep love of the game.

Our mutual appreciation of a sport we both loved, though, is not the most important thing I came to know about Ernie.

Ernie the footballer was one thing, but Ernie the man was just as impressive.

At the time, you see, I was going through a very tough patch in my life, domestically speaking, and the warmth, support and affection he showed really helped me through a difficult experience. That is something I will never forget.

When my father died, the stories people told us of his kindness towards them gave us real comfort as a family. In the same way, I know the Moss family will have been told hundreds of stories, similar to mine regarding my dad, of how Ernie helped them in one way or another.

Now that Ernie has left us, I hope his family and loved ones can draw at least some comfort from what they are told about him, by friends, fans and colleagues alike, for not only was Ernie Moss a great player, he was a warm, kind, beautiful person too.

I count myself lucky to have known him.

John Stiles is the son of Manchester United great and England 1966 World Cup hero Nobby Stiles. His professional playing career took in numerous clubs over the years, not least Shamrock Rovers, Vancouver Whitecaps, Leeds United and Doncaster Rovers. He is the nephew of Republic of Ireland legend Johnny Giles. There is an added poignancy to John's words, as his father fell victim to Alzheimer's disease thought to have been aggravated by repeatedly heading footballs during his illustrious days as a top-flight player.[12]

---

12 https://www.bbc.co.uk/sport/football/54976910

Martin of the *Mail*

Martin Samuel

*'Chesterfield legend Moss was prolific hero
of a bygone era'*

They were called Match Facts. To my knowledge,
the first comprehensive marks out of ten that were
ever awarded to participants in English football. Now
it would be unthinkable to not be told that the left-
back for Norwich was only worth five and the striker
seven, but back then, roughly 40 years ago, it was
groundbreaking.

The publication was a new magazine, *Match
Weekly*, and the collation of all this information across
four divisions was done by Hayters Sports Agency,
where I worked at weekends, while still at school.
Saturday evening, the cramped office upstairs in
Gough Square was given over to copytakers in archaic
headsets, taking down a list of names and numbers
from every game in the country. It was easier then,
because almost all football took place at 3pm on
Saturday, even if Manchester United and Manchester
City were both drawn at home in the FA Cup.

My job was to use the squad lists in the *Rothmans
Football Yearbook* to check for spelling mistakes or

other tiny errors from typists who could hardly be expected to be across every nuance of Exeter City's back four.

It left me with an encyclopaedic knowledge of a specific, brief time in English football. If I hear the name of a player, I can have a fair stab at whether he played for Tranmere Rovers or Halifax Town. Utterly useless, of course, but I know this: Ernie Moss always scored.

At the time for Chesterfield, but then for Port Vale and after that, well, I lost track. I didn't do the ratings shift any more and Moss moved – to Lincoln, to Doncaster, to Stockport, to Rochdale. And back to Chesterfield, of course, where he was as revered as Bobby Charlton at Old Trafford.

He died last week, aged 71, from Pick's disease, a form of dementia brought on, no doubt, by his prodigious talent in the air. All of his clubs, 12 as a player, plus seven more as a coach and manager, paid tribute. All did his memory, as a man and professional, proud.

I don't know if I ever saw him play, but I saw his numbers. No penalties, either. In my imagination, he's rising above two defenders to power home another header at Saltergate.

A true hero of a game long past.

Martin Samuel is a renowned sports journalist who has spent a distinguished career with several outlets, including the Daily Mail *and* The Times, *and wrote this lovely piece shortly after Ernie Moss died. It was published in the* Daily Mail *dated 20 July 2021, and is reproduced here by kind personal permission of Martin.*

. . . .

Terry turns the clock back

Terry Fox

'A kind, considerate person'

I had the privilege of meeting Ernie Moss when I was involved in different kinds of charity work in my role as a trades union secretary with Coalite, who operated a plant at Bolsover.

On one such occasion, Ernie visited in order to hand out prizes to local children, but what is unknown to many people is that he had been doing just that sort of thing for many years, privately and without recognition. That was the way Ernie preferred it; no fuss, no spotlight, just a humble man giving back to his community.

What is also largely unknown is that Ernie also became involved in charitable events to help raise funds for disabled children; again, without drawing attention to his involvement.

I came to recognise him as a son, so to speak, and I developed a deep respect and affection for him as a fine character; a kind, considerate person who had time for everyone.

It broke my heart when I realised Ernie's dementia was taking its toll, especially when I met him once, but he patently had no memory of who I was, and no recollection of the times we had shared together. In fact, he backed away from me, which was sadder than I can put into words. None of that was his fault, of course. The Ernie I knew and loved, to whom I had become a kind of father figure, was never like that at all. All the same, it hurt, and it was a tragic scenario.

I thought he was wonderful.

Terry Fox lives in Chesterfield and was first taken to see his local team play in what he thinks was a semi-final of some kind against Manchester United, shortly after the Second World War. Chesterfield lost 1-0. For many years Terry never missed a match, home or away, enjoying the company of his sons at games. Nowadays, no longer being as young as he was, and with the appearance of a mobility scooter in his life, he doesn't get to see Chesterfield as often as he would like, but he still follows their fortunes as best he can.

. . . .

From the other end of the pitch

Jim Brown

*'He was by far one of the most dangerous
centre-forwards of his era'*

As a somewhat naive 20-year-old leaving my home in
Scotland for the first time, to sign professional terms
as a goalkeeper for Chesterfield, I became a team-
mate of Ernie's and from the very first day of training
realised he was by far the most naturally fit player
I had ever met. I still remember an early training
session at Eckington with manager Jim McGuigan
sending us off on a cross-country run. Immediately,
Ernie was in the lead with everyone else following
on behind.

The bit of that run that sticks in my mind most,
though, is Ernie leading most of the players back past
me before I had reached the halfway point. I well
recall being lapped! At that point, I realised just how
much work I had to do if I was to catch up. (In the end
I never did catch him, no matter how hard I tried.)

Ernie and his wife Jenny, along with Dave Wilson
and his wife Kath, who were neighbours in Walton,
took me under their wing, and I was a regular visitor

to their houses for some good home cooking in their company. I was always made to feel very welcome, which really helped me to settle into my new life a long way from home. That friendship and thoughtfulness is something I will never forget.

Most will agree that Ernie was not the world's most skilful ball player or dribbler, but he was by far one of the most dangerous centre-forwards of his era. A towering target man, he was a danger in the air at corners and free kicks, as well as being very difficult to mark in the box. Ernie could read the game well and had the knack of being in the right place at the right time, particularly around the penalty area, skills which made him a natural goalscorer. I'm sure when the opposition heard the shouts of 'Ernie! Ernie! Ernie!' echoing around the stadium they knew they were in for a difficult day. Ernie was a player who always gave 100 per cent effort. He was a joy to play alongside, and someone you could always rely on as a friend and team-mate. The number of appearances he made, and the number of goals he scored, speak volumes for the man he was.

As a local lad who became a hero for his hometown team, I can't think of anyone who more thoroughly deserves to have a book written about his life and career. It will be a fitting testament to a man who paid a cruel price for all the effort and commitment he gave to every club he played for throughout the years.

I wish Jenny and her family good luck for the future and I'm sure they know the club and our loyal Spireite fans will always be there to support them.

Jim Brown enjoyed a successful career as a goalkeeper, making over 300 appearances in the Football League and playing for four years in the North American Soccer League. Starting out with Albion Rovers, Jim's playing days included two spells with Chesterfield, during which he even managed to score one goal! Jim represented Scotland five times at under-23 level, and gained one full international cap in 1975, in a match against Romania. In retirement, he worked for a time as commercial manager at Chesterfield.

. . . .

Paul's predicament

Paul Lemon

*'Ernie's interest in signing me
made me feel ten feet tall'*

I remember when John Duncan, the manager at the time, was keen to move me on from Chesterfield in 1993 (I headed, briefly, to Telford United and Derry City). Ernie stepped in by trying to sign me for Gainsborough Trinity, where he was manager at the time.

I had never played at non-league level, but as Ernie and I sat in his car chatting over my options, he told me he really wanted me there. Given that I was going through a tough patch, and feeling rejected and unwanted as a footballer, Ernie's interest in signing me made me feel ten feet tall.

The previous six months had been some kind of hell for me, career-wise, but Ernie sold Gainsborough Trinity to me, and made me feel as though I still had something to offer as a player.

My predicament was that I was on £500 a week at Chesterfield, which was decent money back then in the early 1990s, but the most Ernie could offer me, bless his heart, was £85 a week plus expenses for petrol. As my mortgage was costing me £900 a month, there was, unfortunately, no way I could possibly accept the deal. Ernie apologised for the fact that the club couldn't afford any more, but he did at least point out that I would have been one of the best earners at Gainsborough Trinity!

I thanked him, of course, shook his hand, but declined his offer.

The abiding memory of that episode, though, regardless of football itself, was of Ernie Moss trying his best to help out a friend whose confidence had taken a knock and who was in need of some support, emotionally and financially.

A native of Middlesbrough, Paul Lemon played in midfield for Sunderland, making 107 league appearances for the club. His playing career encompassed multiple other clubs, including Chesterfield, for whom he played 85 league games. Having previously scouted for the likes of Sheffield United and Huddersfield Town, Paul was employed as chief scout at Chesterfield until 2021, overseeing this important part of the club's recruiting network. He greatly enjoys his friendship with the Moss family.

. . . .

Susan says

Susan Cornthwaite

'It's so much more than just friendship'

Unfortunately, I'm too young to have ever watched Ernie actually play, but I have grown up hearing such great things about the footballer he was.

I was fortunate enough to meet Ernie's family, becoming a friend of his daughter, Sarah, while my own daughter Sophie became best friends with one of Ernie's granddaughters, Callie.

It was so much more than just friendship, though. Ernie was such a big family man that people he grew to know and love were treated as part of his family. For example, I remember sitting in his living room on the sofa holding his hand, watching a game show or something like that on television, and, more often than not, me getting the answers wrong while Ernie got them right!

You could never leave Ernie's house without a kiss on the cheek and a wave from the window, and even when Ernie tragically began to lose his power of speech, the look of love in his eyes and the trademark smile on his face was always enough; he didn't need words in order to communicate.

There never was a truer gentleman than the mighty Ernie Moss, and he will always hold a special place within my heart.

Susan Cornthwaite is a married mum of two and has been an avid Chesterfield fan and season ticket holder for over 20 years, attending matches home and away with her mother, who herself used to attend games with her own father (Susan's grandad). Sadly, since Susan's mum passed away in 2011, she doesn't go along to as many games as she used to, as it 'just doesn't feel the same'. She does, though, still keep a close eye on the scores.

. . . .

Darryl's diary

Darryl Carpenter

'Ernie Moss was revered and respected like no other player who donned the blue of Chesterfield'

My first proper recollection of Ernie was watching Chesterfield's youth team win the Northern Intermediate League Cup. My dad said the 'beanpole' Ernie was a local lad and played for the Tube Works, which meant nothing to me at the time. He won everything in the air and seemed to score goals off every part of his frame, and scuffed a few as well. The boy with the Beatles haircut was never particularly elegant throughout his career, but, boy, was he effective.

My next real 'Ernie moment' came when he scored all four goals in an early season 4-0 demolition of Newport County, in what would become the famous

1969/70 promotion season. His exploits were even mentioned on *Match of the Day* – imagine that today! Ernie was a raw talent but developed very quickly that season and formed a unique partnership with Kevin Randall (another of my heroes).

Enough has been written about this giant and Town legend over the years, so rather than talk about his longevity and goalscoring exploits with Town and many other teams, I'll keep my Ernie memories to specific games.

For example, I remember one game on Boxing Day 1970, away to Rotherham United. Arriving late (as was Dad's wont at that time!), we ended up on the Tivoli End with the locals and witnessed Ernie produce a sensational overhead kick winner. Initially, we stood silent among the Rotherham fans, who were as stunned as we were by Moss's acrobatics. The best we could do was stand and applaud!

During Ernie's second spell with Chesterfield he finally broke Herbert Munday's club goalscoring record. To do it on a Tuesday night at Bramall Lane was extra special!

Whenever supporters use the phrase 'Mr Chesterfield', there is never any doubt who they are talking about. Ernie Moss was a humble, decent man who gave his life to football, his family and his town.

I can't fail to raise a smile every time I think of him, and whenever I go into the foyer at the ground and look at the mosaic showing him climbing majestically to head the ball, the feeling is priceless.[13]

Years after Ernie's playing days came to an end (in fact, even to this day), fans of a certain vintage will say 'Mossy would have buried that' if and when a cross into the box has been spurned. Such is his lasting influence on my club and local people who follow the game. Youngsters born years after the great man stopped playing know who Ernie Moss was and what he will always mean to the very soul and fabric of this corner of north Derbyshire.

My final thought on Ernie relates to the Moss & Miller sports shop in Brampton. With my school friends, I would often call in on the way into town from William Rhodes School. We would look in at the window to make sure Ernie was working there, rather than Geoff (sorry, Geoff!). If he was, we would troop in and spend ages with him talking football, cricket and all things.

Those memories will last forever. He greeted us schoolkids with a beaming smile and, 'Hey up, lads.'

---

13 See Robert Lally's page https://rialtoceramix.co.uk/

Even though he knew we were unlikely to actually buy much, or even anything at all, Ernie always welcomed us in to chew the fat.

Ernie Moss was revered and respected like no other player who donned the blue of Chesterfield FC.

I consider myself so fortunate to have seen him play hundreds of games, scoring plenty of goals in the process, and to have spent time in his company. He rightly had a road named after him[14] and although he battled a terrible illness, my image of the great man will never dim.

Ernie! Ernie! Ernie!

Born and bred a Spireite, Darryl Carpenter has been watching Chesterfield since 1967. He has followed his club all across the country, attending hundreds of games with his parents. Darryl supported the Chesterfield Football Supporters' Society as secretary, and now, in retirement, helps out the Chesterfield FC Community Trust, carrying on a family tradition of helping the club that dates back to the 1920s.

---

14 Ernie Moss Way in Chesterfield, adjacent to the Technique Stadium.

Week after week with Wilkinson

Alan Wilkinson

*'I feel privileged to have
spent time with him'*

Ernie was my all-time favourite CFC player, closely followed by Kevin Randall, I have to say. Watching him play week after week was an absolute pleasure, especially celebrating every goal from my place on the Kop.

Likewise, watching Ernie, Kevin and Chesterfield away from home too.

Ernie Moss was such an inspiration that I always wanted to play up front, trying to emulate him, but that didn't materialise and I ended up playing as a keeper.

In my eyes Ernie carries legendary status here at CFC, and always will. No one will come close. He had such a presence as a player.

When I went to work at Chesterfield-based radio station Peak FM I was sent to interview him one day, so I turned up at Moss & Miller as agreed. We went upstairs and I froze. Here I was, looking at the man who had been my hero for years, and I was actually getting to interview him face-to-face, in person!

Those radio interviews became a weekly thing, every Thursday, which is how I got to know Ernie Moss the man as well as Ernie Moss the player. He also summarised many games for me on Peak FM, and his summaries were always fun, witty and thoroughly enjoyable. I came to realise just what a humble person he was, and very friendly with it. Over the years, I also came to know Ernie's wife and daughters, and they really did make me so welcome as part of an extended family.

On another note, I bought my first media bag at the shop. It was priced at a tenner, but Ernie said he would knock something off for me if I bought it. True to his word, he did just that – and sold me the bag for £9.99!

Ernie was indeed a legend and a gentleman and more than that, he became a good mate. I feel privileged to have spent time with him, and I can't thank Jenny, Nikki and Sarah enough for making me feel part of their family. I could go on for a long time!

Ernie you were a star, and as Dionne Warwick (I think!) once sang, thank you for being a friend.

Love you, Ernie. X

Alan Wilkinson worked at Peak FM for five years on Back of the Net, *featuring live commentary of Chesterfield's games, before moving on to Spire Radio and then Elastic FM. He has been a devoted Spireite since 1963, 'through thick and thin'.*

. . . .

Matt's memories

Matt Fletcher

'He will always have legendary status at Gainsborough Trinity Football Club'

All I can say is that during his time as manager at Gainsborough Trinity, Ernie Moss built a quality attacking team, one that played with no fear.

Ernie attracted enormous respect from the players in that team, and from the supporters. It was obvious, every time we played, that every member of the Trinity squad simply wanted to play for him.

I had the privilege of attending the UniBond League Cup Final when Gainsborough Trinity beat Boston, which was an amazing experience, particularly as Trinity fans almost filled the venue for that game, Lincoln City's Sincil Bank.

Ernie gave us fans confidence and hope that we could be one of the best non-league teams around, and because of that he will always have legendary status at Gainsborough Trinity Football Club.

Road opening with family – Nikki, Georgia, Fin and Erin

Proud moment

True love

Ernie at opening of Ernie Moss Way

Fans gather to say their farewells

Ernie playing at Wembley Stadium with Johnny Quinn's All-Stars in the Cup Final

Happy times

Ernie with his girls, Nikki and Sarah

Team-mates

Young Ernie

Winning Derbyshire Senior Cup with Matlock Town FC

Last game at Saltergate with Nikki and Sarah, wearing Dad's shirts

Ernie with his Testimonial football

Young love –
December 1971

Matt Fletcher was raised in Gainsborough and has been an ardent supporter of Gainsborough Trinity since around 1994/95, just as he was first becoming interested in football. Matt says, 'If it wasn't for Trinity I probably wouldn't have got into football as much as I did.'

. . . .

Training with Tony

Tony Brien

'What a legend'

Just reminiscing here.

I was a 19-year-old kid walking into the dressing room when I signed for Town for the first time. The first face I saw was Ernie. I commented that I thought he had retired. His reply was so typical of his attitude, 'I have, Tony, but I still train with the lads to keep fit.'

Ernie Moss got me my first pair of boots from his sports shop, on the house. What a kind and generous gesture.

What a legend.

I am so sad he is no longer with us.

Tony Brien, born in Dublin, enjoyed a footballing career as a defender with Leicester City, Chesterfield, Rotherham

United, West Bromwich Albion, Mansfield Town, Chester City and Hull City. Perhaps best remembered for his time with Chesterfield, Tony represented the club 204 times at senior level, scoring eight goals in the process.

. . . .

Peter's pastimes

Peter Grainger

'I had nothing but admiration for him'

Ernie and I were good friends from roughly 1964 to 1968. We used to play football and cricket on the local green every Sunday, come rain or shine, with other local kids and lads from villages two or three miles away, making our own goalposts and netting. Football was definitely the highlight of the week!

Saturdays were taken up with collecting prized autographs at nearby grounds such as Bramall Lane (Sheffield United), Hillsborough (Sheffield Wednesday), the Baseball Ground (Derby County), the City Ground (Nottingham Forest), and occasionally Old Trafford (Ernie was a big fan of Manchester United). If we weren't hanging about outside the grounds, we would gather at the hotels where the teams were staying.

One particular memory of my friendship with Ernie in those bygone days stands out. On the day of the 1966 World Cup Final, I went on holiday to Scarborough with Ernie, his parents, his sister Jennie and her friend (not great timing!). Anxious not to miss the game, though, Ernie and I went off in search of a shop where we could watch England play West Germany through the window! Thankfully, we found a television rental shop and stood outside from 2pm until the celebrations ended. Good times!

In later years, my friend Ernie took a Saturday job at Burton's and after starting to play football for Tube Works he was eventually talent-spotted and taken on Chesterfield's books. The rest, as they say, is history.

Unfortunately, Ernie and I somehow lost touch with each other when he was playing or training most days and when he started courting. I used to go to Saltergate to watch him play but I don't think we actually spoke for over 50 years; not because of any falling-out, I hasten to add, as I had nothing but admiration for him. He was a really friendly guy and a good mate. I was really sad to hear of his illness, and now I wish his family all the best.

Peter Grainger was born in 1948 and although he and Ernie went to different schools, he seems to recall being

*introduced to Ernie through football or possibly when
groups of friends met up at Friday night 'picture shows'.*

. . . .

Andrew's anecdotes

Andrew Cratchley

*'Ernie always stopped to say hello to people
and was genuinely interested in them'*

I have tried many times to put into words how
special Ernie was to us, and how special Jenny and
the Moss family still are to us, and were to my mum
and dad. Dad became Ernie's friend in the 1980s and
later would travel with him when he was managing,
particularly while at Gainsborough Trinity.

Ernie celebrating the 1969/70 championship
success in front of the main stand at Saltergate seems
to be one of my earliest footballing memories. Ernie
has provided so many memorable moments, though,
that it is hard to choose just a few! Like many other
fans, I remember his classic headers, his hat-trick on
the losing side at Walsall and his trademark (typically
understated) celebration.

Imagine my surprise, then, coming home from
town on the last bus one Saturday night, only to find

the man himself in our front room, poring over one of Dad's many programmes and recalling the fixture in question in some detail, then going to find another programme and game to recount, while Mum and Jenny had another cup of tea (or glass of red!). This became a regular feature of Saturday nights as Mum, Dad, Ernie and Jenny became good friends.

I was lucky enough to get to know them both, and I am perhaps one of few fans who has actually been watched by Ernie, when he and Dad came to Leeds one Saturday afternoon (presumably without a proper game to go to!) to see me playing in a match. Sadly, I didn't get on the scoresheet in that game, but we won so on that occasion there was no need to ask Ernie to quickly put his boots on and lend a hand!

One of my team-mates, a York City fan, recognised Ernie and was in deep conversation with him after the game. Similarly, once, when visiting a friend who supported Peterborough United, I mentioned that Ernie was a friend of Dad's and the guy said Ernie was a favourite although he had only spent a short time at Posh. As I knew Ernie was at Mum and Dad's that afternoon, I rang them and Ernie spoke to my friend for a good half an hour; typical of the man, he was always willing to talk football.

A further recollection is of playing cricket a couple of times with the big man, even sharing in a century stand with him on a difficult Sunday afternoon, though it needs to be said I only mustered about 20 runs of our combined total!

We lived in New Zealand for a while and when I came home after a couple of years, Dad said he would pick me up from Heathrow. I was worried as he wasn't in the best of health, but it turned out to be no problem. I had a top-quality chauffeur and after quick hellos the conversation for the next three hours was about games Ernie had played in that Dad had watched, or current players (who might make the grade and who might not), while I dozed in the back.

The new stadium meant Dad could go to games again. The three of us had tickets in the Legends Lounge and it was always a great afternoon to look forward to, Ernie with a cup of tea, Dad with a pint of lager and me somewhere in between. Ernie always stopped to say hello to people and was genuinely interested in them.

Sadly, Dad's health deteriorated and the last game we all went to together was the championship-winning game against Fleetwood in 2014. Ernie was also not so good and to me it really was the end of a fantastic few years. It was, though, great to see Ernie with Nikki and Sarah and their families at the matches and this kept me going to home games, when perhaps, sometimes, to be honest, the performances didn't!

Jenny remained a great friend and support to Mum and over 50 years on from that first memory, I am truly grateful for the family friendship. Ernie was a genuine man, not just on the field but off it too; a gentleman, a husband, a father, a friend and a hero to many. Truly, he was a Spireite legend.

Andrew Cratchley was born in Clay Cross, Derbyshire, in the same house in which his father and sister were also born. His parents lived in Cutthorpe, a small village near Chesterfield, for over 40 years, and Andrew's claim to fame is that his grandmother delivered Dennis Skinner (the Labour MP for Bolsover from 1970 to 2019) into this world. Andrew is a Spireite at heart, despite, as he admits, 'dalliances with Nottingham Forest and Leeds United'.

. . . .

An unedited Ukrainian

Volodymyr Holod and Phil Tooley

'Ernie was the town's biggest hero'

Volodymyr Holod contributed this fascinating article in his second language, and I have chosen to include it, largely unedited. This is out of respect for Volodymyr's excellent contribution, but also because there is a certain charm about reading his words as they were originally sent to me. I hope you agree.

Embedded within Volodymyr's contribution is an excellent piece from Phil Tooley, who can quite comfortably be described as a Chesterfield super fan! Phil is the kind of supporter every club wishes they had, and I make no apology for referring you to a website that tells a little of his story. Such fans represent the backbone of lower league football, and I warmly commend this link to you: http:// spireitestrust.org.uk/2017/11/06/phil-tooley-celebrates-40th-year-volunteer/. Chesterfield fan Mark Barton is also quoted in Volodymyr's article.

My journey as a Ukrainian Spireite started in 2016, I was just looking for a new team to play in *FIFA* – but little did I know that my new virtual team will became my favourite one in the real life!

Following CFC in social media, as well as talking to my first Spireite friends and reading about the club's history, I fell in love with the club. I honestly can say that this experience was an eye-opener for me. This unique community spirit captured my attention, and I became a part of a big Spireites family.

One of the fundamental things in my supporting of Chesterfield was exploring the club's history, from collecting old programmes to watching old videos; from reading special articles to listening to elder supporters' stories. Very soon I've learned that the club has a lot of prominent players, from Herbert Munday, who played for CFC over 100 years ago, to Jack Lester. Even so, there was one player that overshadowed everyone. That person was Ernie Moss. Known as a humble family man, he was the town's biggest hero. Let me (and the people that knew Ernie closer) tell you his story.

Born locally in 1949, Ernie was a clerk in the Derbyshire County Council education offices at Matlock before joining Chesterfield FC in April 1967. He made his debut the next year, scoring one goal in 17 appearances. His second professional season brought him first league success as Chesterfield won the Fourth Division title. Ernie netted 20 goals to help his club to promote that season. In the Third Division the striker continued to do his job, scoring 74 goals in 210 appearances before being sold to Peterborough United in 1975.

After the brief spell with the 'Posh', Ernie moved to Mansfield Town to enjoy his 15 matches in the Second Division. In 1978, he returned to Saltergate, helping his original club to avoid relegation by just four points. The next two seasons were quite successful, in both of them Chesterfield were close to promotion and, most notably, the Spireites won Anglo-Scottish Cup in 1981.

After this success, Ernie Moss moved to Port Vale, where he won player of the year award in 1982. In 1983, Ernie moved to Lincoln City, where he played just 11 games before joining Doncaster Rovers and finishing second in the Fourth Division. In 1984, however, he returned to Chesterfield to help his club in promotion battle of 1984/85 season. The Spireites won promotion, so Ernie had a chance to play some Third Division football for almost next two seasons. That was the last time he played for Chesterfield.

From 1986, Ernie played for Stockport County, Scarborough, Rochdale and Kettering Town. Ernie's 17 goals helped Kettering to become Football Conference runners-up in 1989. After this success, he played for Matlock Town and Shepshed Charterhouse. Ernie ended his playing career in Kettering Town in 1992.

In 1992, Ernie Moss started his career in football management. He became an assistant manager in Boston United. Three years later, he was appointed as a manager in Gainsborough Trinity. Later, he managed Leek Town, Gainsborough Trinity for the second time, Matlock Town, Hucknall Town and Belper Town.

In 2014, Ernie was diagnosed with Pick's disease (a rare form of dementia). Now his family had to try to help him and to raise awareness of footballers' professional illnesses.

We took a brief look on Ernie Moss's career, but the main question remains unanswered; what makes him such a special person for Chesterfield? Phil Tooley, a lifelong Spireite and a volunteer for CFC for over 40 years, will help us to find the answer:

'There are too many legends about these days, and rest assured, not many of them are real legends,' says Phil. 'They'll soon be forgotten by those conferring the title when the next temporary star comes along. But Ernie Moss was a real legend, and he'll be remembered long after the transitory title-holders have been and gone. Always a Chesterfield resident, Ernie came to Saltergate and then the new stadium whenever he could, always willing to share a story or two, always just quite wondering why supporters loved him so much. It was always the team for him, never just the famous number eight.

'Stars have become superstars and megastars, many of them are just mercenaries who'll say and do the right things because that's the best way to enhance their standing. Ernie didn't fall into that category. He was a regular bloke, working his hardest at a job he was good at, to get better. He got better at it, he helped countless teams to improve and he did it all without any fuss and without wanting anything special, with substantial amounts of his success coming in the town he was born in and always lived in.

'Super legend? Nah. Mega legend? Nah. It was just Ernie, everyone in Chesterfield knows exactly what that means and exactly what status that man held. In football *Top Trumps*, Ernie topped them all.'

In fact, it isn't easy to add something more to these words, especially when one lifelong Spireite describes another. Nevertheless, Ernie had another significant role in his life: he was a great dad for his daughters.

'When we were small, we didn't understand Dad's popularity, he was our dad, and we were a close family unit,' explains Ernie's daughter Nikki. 'We knew Dad was a footballer, but that didn't register as anything out of the ordinary. Our lives were based around football, so we knew Dad had a game on Saturday, that he trained every day, cleaned his boots every Saturday morning, but that was our life, our normal. We never felt pushed out by his job, we went to all the home games and cheered him on. When he scored, he would always look up into the stand at us and wave. That was special.'

'Dad was first and foremost a family man who just happened to be lucky enough to do the only job he ever dreamed of,' adds Ernie's daughter Sarah. 'Obviously he wasn't always around because of training and matches, but we never missed out. We went to every home game possible, from being born, and when Dad was at home with us, we all did things together as a family ... walking the dog, gardening, watching footy on TV, playing board games, etc. By the way, we had the free run of Saltergate, which I guess we didn't appreciate at the time. We played on the pitch after every match and went in the changing rooms, physio room and even the boardroom!'

Now both Ernie's daughters admit that they only realised their dad's significance when he ended his career.

'As a teenager I became more aware of Dad's fame but he always called himself a "leg end" (not legend) and was so modest. It was only upon speaking about his illness and arranging charity events for him I have fully understood his fame, and the high esteem and love people had for him,' says Nikki.

'As to Dad being a star, I do feel that now. Chesterfield FC fans literally adored Dad, but as a child I guess I didn't fully understand how famous he was,' explains Sarah.

Sarah and Nikki had to fight with their dad's Pick's disease. 'It took away everything, apart from my memories,' explains Sarah. 'I truly believe football caused this to Dad's brain, but even so I also know that Dad wouldn't change his football career for the world. It's the only thing (apart from marrying my mum Jenny, the love of his life and have a family) he ever wanted to do and he would have played for nothing.

'That said, though, the footballing world needs to address it as far too many men are dying for a job they literally gave their lives for. The only thing that gives me any peace is that I know Dad was sort of happy in his own little world. Unfortunately it's my mum who paid the price as she grieved her husband, in a way, while he was still actually alive.'

Nikki agrees with her sister and insists on action from the football authorities. 'Having to see Dad fade with this disease has destroyed me. Seeing my mum devastated by the loss of her soulmate is harrowing. The football community has been amazing. The fans, the clubs and ex-team-mates all supported Dad and our family, but the football authorities have been neglectful to their former players – that is putting it politely!

'If the PFA had acted when Jeff Astle died, then provisions would have been put in place to help these former players, specialist care available, education and information available, preventative measures put in place, but nothing was done and it has taken many, many more deaths, many more players with dementia or brain illnesses, many more broken families speaking out to get some action finally. A government investigation, concussion subs, information to clubs and players; a small step in a giant problem.'

Now Nikki and Sarah are doing their best to make sure that the whole of England pays attention to the problem of dementia in footballers, in Ernie's memory. Even when he was unable to speak, 'Big Ernie' still was in the centre of the town's discussion. His career brought a lot of glorious memories for everyone, so people want to remember him in some way as a sort of repayment.

'I'm sure we'll have a statue of him one day.[15] The fact no one would pick anyone else shows how much he's loved,' says lifelong Spireite Mark Barton. 'He felt like our talisman, he was always a player opposing fans could name as being associated with us ... one of our own. Ernie fitted the club; unglamorous and

---

15 See page 188 for information regarding the Ernie Moss Memorial Campaign.

never perfect, but he was ours and we loved him just for being himself.'

I may have never seen him playing, but I still know that he was a hero. In fact, a lot of younger Spireites never saw him playing, but Ernie remains Ernie in local folklore as a role model of a footballer and a gentleman. When the entire town cherished a football player like this, you certainly know he should be a special one.

Ernie Moss epitomised that classic English football at lower level. Without glamour, without high salaries, but with passion, with a whole heart, with dedication to the community. As Mark Barton puts it, Ernie was a great example of a bygone era.

Sometimes local hero means way more than the most prominent football stars. Stars are just bright stars. They don't belong to anyone, while people like Ernie Moss are a part of our own world. They give us all they can every Saturday. Football is about that rare sense of belonging to our community. Maybe, this is why we still care about the game.

My name is Volodymyr Holod. I was born in Lviv, western Ukraine. I spent whole my life in my home city or closely around it. Since my childhood, I was interested in football and football programmes. In my 16, I started to do matchday programmes for our local handball club. Since then, I had a lot of great memories including master's degree in Slavic philology. But this achievement can't even compete with becoming a Spireite in 2016. It was certainly one of the highlights in my life. Now I'm a proud Spireite. Ernie Moss reminded me of my grandad. I had very close bond with my grandad Myroslav, and I can partly understand Sarah and Nikki in their situation. My grandad was a miner in our region and then became town mayor. Ernie was my equivalent of Grandad Myroslav in Chesterfield. Ernie had similar roles in his life. He served his community and was a brilliant dad and husband. I never saw Ernie, but only great person can stay in hearts of everyone who knew him. He was a legend of my club and I want to say him 'Thank you' for making Chesterfield a better place during his career and after it, because Ernie Moss is still a synonym to Chesterfield Football Club.

. . . .

Purdy's players

Geraldine Purdy

'A lovely gentleman'

I can always remember when I lived in Walton, and walked to school at Boythorpe, then when I started work in Chesterfield I used to see Ernie taking his Labrador dog for a walk in the morning. Ernie always had time to say hello and chat. A fantastic footballer and a lovely gentleman.

Wonderful memories.

Geraldine Purdy (née Wass) first became interested in football and in Chesterfield in particular, thanks to chats and conversations with Ernie Moss. Living in Walton, a suburb of Chesterfield, Geraldine came to know a few of the players as the club rented a few houses there for temporary accommodation. Originally attending matches at Saltergate, Geraldine nowadays lives near the Technique Stadium and goes there regularly with her husband, daughter and son.

. . . .

A smile from Stan

Stan McTighe

'Ernie knocks in the rebound'

There is one thing that sticks in my memory about Ernie.

Making my way to matches, I used to walk past Cross Street Baptist Chapel. On the billboard outside the church there was a big notice which proclaimed 'Jesus Saves', underneath which someone had added, in bold writing, 'And Ernie Moss knocks in the rebound'.

No offence intended, of course. More a reflection on the affection in which Ernie Moss was (and is) held in the town.

Stan McTighe simply describes himself as 'a Spireite always'.

. . . .

Mr Maris and his missus

Ian Maris

'I can't speak highly enough of the man'

My Ernie story just shows you what a good guy he was. I had my 40th birthday party in August 2001 at the Miners' Arms on Brimington Common. We basically took the whole pub over for the night, with about 100 guests in attendance.

The lady who was my wife at the time was very good at organising party games etc., so we were anticipating a good evening. In those days, there was a popular television show called *They Think It's All Over,* a sort of light-hearted sports quiz show that featured a 'Feel the Sportsman' round. Blindfolded contestants had to 'feel' the sporting celebrity standing in front of them, trying to guess who it was, rather like a security guard would pat down someone going through an airport, say.

I was the last contestant to have a go at the round, and I managed to guess the first two mates quite easily. The last person who was put in front of me, though, I hadn't a clue who it was, and it took me ages feeling around the guy.

Funnily enough, I had a particular habit of just saying 'Ernie Moss' at random if ever I couldn't remember someone's name, and this came in handy that evening. I took a wild guess, and as I was already a huge fan of his anyway, I just shouted out, 'Not got a clue who it is; Ernie Moss!' And it was!

The background to that story is that my missus, knowing how much I admired the bloke, had gone into the Moss & Miller sports shop to ask Ernie if he would turn up as a guest at my party. He said he didn't really do that sort of thing, but my missus being the person she was, sat down in the shop and said, 'I'm not leaving until you agree to it!' So eventually Ernie said he'd turn up for a few minutes on condition she donated £50 to a charity. The deal was struck!

Ernie kept to his side of the bargain, a certain charity was £50 up on the deal, and everyone enjoyed an hour or so in Ernie's company. He chatted to everyone, signed a few autographs, and made my night.

He was such a nice bloke and I can't speak highly enough of the man.

Ian Maris is now retired, after working in IT 'for 30-odd years', at Kennings initially at Brampton, and then HSBC in Sheffield. At the time of this story, he was married to Rachel and lived next door to the Miners' Arms, the pub referred to. He is now married to Ann and living in Woodthorpe. Ian has been a Chesterfield fan all his life, with the first game he went to being a friendly against the Italian side Lanerossi Vicenza in 1970.

. . . .

The key to success

Chris Key

'I was really starstruck when he knocked on the door!'

When I was about 11 years old I played junior football and my dad arranged for Ernie Moss to come and see me as I needed some new football boots (I think

Ernie had just set up his shop with Geoff Miller at the time).

I was a big fan of Chesterfield FC and was really starstruck when he knocked on the door with about five or six pairs of boots!

He was an absolute gentleman and spent ages helping me while I decided which pair to have (I think they were Mitre boots).

In the very next game I played in, I scored the winning goal with my shiny black new boots!

Chris Key has been a Chesterfield supporter all his life. In his younger days he played for Chesterfield Boys and Lady Hardwick Sports, based in Clay Cross, and a few years ago also coached his son's junior football team. Chris continues to enjoy watching both amateur and professional football.

. . . .

Biggs' biggest hero

Alan Biggs

'Ernie Moss – an absolute pleasure and privilege to have watched and known you'

Ernie Moss, where to start? He was my first football hero and is still my biggest. Biggest in every sense actually. In physique and, even more so, in size of heart. A player who wore that heart on his sleeve and had it stamped on a forehead that towered and jutted, propelling some of the most magnificent goals of their type.

Looking back now, those memories feel like a guilty pleasure because of the unacceptable and deeply sad sacrifice Ernie ultimately made in scoring those thundering headers. Little realised at the time, of course, either by him or the supporters who thrilled at his majestic power in the air.

But, having had the pleasure of coming to know the man from his later career at Chesterfield and elsewhere, he would still have thrust that head in where it hurts, giving everything without compromise or regret.

This was a player with the most honest of rough edges. A fierce but fair competitor. And, above all, one with whom most of us who have tried to kick a ball and failed could thoroughly identify, unlike those gifted individuals with sublime natural talent.

Ernie was no genius. Couldn't have been further from it. He told me once, with typical candour and modesty, that when he started he couldn't trap the proverbial bag of cement. But boy, could he head it. That same bag of cement if necessary.

As a teenage Spireite, I recall being infuriated with him at times. It's a myth that he was always a crowd favourite, never getting stick from the crowd. As a gangly, lanky youngster, he was in the most exposed position, playing at the sharp end where a miscontrol, heavy touch or scuffed shot would end a promising attack and bring howls of derision.

He looked ungainly but took it all uncomplainingly, never hiding away, just trying harder.

Playing as the hold-up man with his back to goal, things didn't always stick with Ernie. But he had bagfuls of application and persistence as he worked tirelessly at his game under an intuitive manager in Jim McGuigan, to become a striker you wouldn't swap for anybody.

His limitations became fewer but fans learned to accept them anyway to focus on his strengths. These I saw for the first time in the 1968/69 season when Chesterfield, with Ernie already a first-team fledging, won the Northern Intermediate League Cup. He headed a trademark goal in the final if I recall correctly.

I remember from earlier, in late 1968, what could well have been his first senior goal at Saltergate. Certainly among his first. It was in an FA Cup first round tie with Skelmersdale United.

It's odd but I can still picture that goal very precisely.

The Skelmersdale keeper misdirected a throw-out straight to Kevin Randall, who, of course, was to become a wonderful strike partner. Kevin's shot was parried sideways by the embarrassed keeper and Ernie slid in to roll the ball home.

He was often on the spot just like that and it wasn't just a story of glorious headers. Ernie was a specialist with the overhead kick.

One that stands out was late in the Fourth Division promotion season of 1969/70. In front of 16,000 at Saltergate, Chesterfield were leading rivals Wrexham 1-0 (a long-ranger from Tom Fenoughty) when the famous corner routine of that era worked its magic once more.

John Archer's flag kick was flicked on at the near post and Ernie, finding himself slightly ahead of the ball, arced backwards to flip the ball into the net over his shoulder and secure a vital victory. I was in the crowd in a ferment behind that goal.

An even better example was the following season in the Third Division when, in front of a 14,000 local derby throng at Millmoor, Ernie's spectacular overhead kick was the winner in a 2-1 triumph over Rotherham United.

But the headers were his hallmark. One that is indelibly clear for me was a diving, torpedo-like effort that won an FA Cup replay with Barnsley in the 1970/71 season. I was standing right behind it in a crowd of 13,000 as the ball ripped into the roof of the net.

At this time, the mighty Moss man was a distant idol for a schoolboy, only diffidently addressed once when I dared ask him a question at a supporters' forum in the town. I didn't listen to the answer, conscious only that the great man was talking, and talking to me!

More relevant was that Moss attended the event on crutches, despite having suffered a serious injury that ruled him out for the rest of the season. That was typical of his public-spiritedness and team ethic; reasons beyond football why he was loved.

Later I came to know him, and it was easy. My early career, becoming sports editor at Radio Hallam, put me in gloriously close contact with the club I'd supported since my family moved north from Kent.

Ernie was a willing interviewee, always speaking sense and unfailingly genuine. In those days, it was possible for reporters to travel on the team coach on the odd occasion and I'll never forget Ernie taking the time and trouble to both involve and look after me on a trip to Reading. He was the life and soul of that party, leading the way with jokes and general merriment.

So it's not just the player I recall with so much affection, though that would have been enough.

They say you should never meet your heroes but Ernie has proved the lie to that. He's been everything and more you'd want him to be. Honest as a player, honest as a man. A powerful performer but, in a sporting and life sense, gentle with it.

Ernie Moss, an absolute pleasure and privilege to have watched and known you, sir. You were a credit to football and your family.

Alan Biggs follows the fortunes of Chesterfield and a host of other clubs in his role as a football journalist and broadcaster, working at this time of writing as a reporter for talkSPORT. Alan has worked within the realm of national radio and television for several decades, and has written regularly in both local and national newspapers.

. . . .

A sonnet from Stu

Stu Middleton

'A gentleman with a Spireite history'

Our Ernie

On January 10th it's Ernie Moss Day,

Many Spireites have memories of his play;

I firmly believe 'Our Ernie' deserves an honourable statue,

Special recognition for our number eight in Spireite blue.

OK, as a Stag[16] he helped them win promotion,

But he soon returned home, therefore ending the commotion;

Repeated the promotion feat with Vale and Doncaster too,

But 'Our Ernie' always remained a loyal Blue.

In 539 appearances he scored quite a lot,

Yet not one did he score from the penalty spot!

He led from the front, scored most with his head,

Yes 'Our Ernie' was a leader, he wasn't easily led.

Sadly, now Ernie has a more personal fight

So turn up, sing his name loud, give Ernie some delight.

Ernie! Ernie! Ernie! was the much heralded cry,

I guess on Saturday, grown men will have a tear in their eye.

---

16 Mansfield Town, Chesterfield's arch rivals, are nicknamed the Stags.

Not so much a fallen hero, but a gentleman with a
    Spireite history
Come on, Spireites, fill the Proact, show Ernie's
    memory some dignity.[17]

Stu Middleton describes himself as 'a Spireite through and through'. Ernie Moss was his first hero in blue, so much so that when the news of his horrible illness first came to light, he wrote a poem in honour of Ernie, to coincide with Ernie Moss Day at the Technique Stadium. Stu sent this poem, along with a photograph of him and his son meeting Ernie one day, to Ernie's daughter, Sarah.

. . . .

Gordon goes on

Gordon Harding

'One hundred per cent every time he pulled the shirt on'

My first association with Ernie came about when we were team-mates with Staveley Welfare Juniors cricket team, winning the league and cup double a few years ago now. Ernie was a pretty handy fast bowler, while

---

17 This poetic tribute was submitted before Ernie Moss died, but it is published unedited because it refers to a special, specific day in the club's history.

I was nippy in the outfield, could catch and throw! In the cup final that season, played at Grassmoor, we were going for the double, we scored an abysmal 80-something. After only half their allotted overs, our opponents, Killamarsh were within 20 runs of victory with all wickets intact. The match was well and truly on!

Cue a bit of hostile bowling from Ernie, and wicketkeeper Alan Stevenson, and the tide slowly but surely began to turn. Wickets tumbled and the Killamarsh run rate slowed significantly. At a point of high cricketing drama, Ernie was saved for the final ferocious over, and in dialogue with our captain, started setting the field. As I was about to head for the square leg boundary, Ernie called me over, telling me he wanted me at silly mid-off, tight in on the batsman, telling me to 'intimidate him'.

The thing was, I stood about 5ft 7in, weighing in at a maximum of seven stone wet through. Intimidation wasn't, therefore, my forte! However, doing as I was told and dutifully standing way too near the batsman, I looked round and noticed Ernie nodding approvingly. After each nerve-wracking delivery, Ernie motioned me to encroach ever further into the batsman's airspace.

We were in touching distance of the trophy, even though I was in ever-increasing danger of being struck with a bat. Then this was it: one ball left, three runs to win!

Ernie nodded one final time; I crouched, hands on knees, raising them slightly as I heard Ernie's foot slam on to the bowling crease. The battered ball whizzed past my right ear and in a millisecond headed back at me via the bat.

Nestled safely in my hand was a scalding meteorite. I couldn't tell whether it had bounced first or not, but the wicketkeeper collected my throw and flattened the stumps anyway, and it was over! Much jubilation followed, and as we hauled ourselves off the pitch, Ernie put his arm round me and with a big grin said, 'See, a bit of intimidation works!'

True enough, I played my part, and I am proud of that, but in reality it was Ernie that won that day. He saw something in me that I didn't know existed, and brought it out for the team.

Forward a few short years to the Chantry Youth Club at Middlecroft, and Ernie had just broken into the first team at Chesterfield, as a replacement for the much-worshipped Ivan Hollett, who claimed a highly respectable tally of 62 goals in 157 appearances for Chesterfield; a hard act to follow.

It seems amazing now, in the era of modern football, even to picture a professional footballer going to a youth club, but that's how it was back then, sometimes even after a midweek fixture!

Ernie's first games were hard for him, following in Ivan's footsteps. The goals weren't coming and the fans sometimes became fickle and impatient, giving him some stick from the terraces.

Supporters can be notorious for that, even though nobody could fault Ernie for his enthusiasm. After one particular home game, though, a very humbled Ernie trudged into the club, and a few of us gathered round for the post-match debate. Try as we might, it was hard to lift his spirits, he was a bit exasperated, and the ball just wouldn't go in the net. And to make matters worse cries of 'Ivan! Ivan!' were heard from a contingent of the Kop.[18]

All eyes turned to me, a known 'Koppite', and questioned if I had joined in. 'Absolutely not,' was my reply. 'No,' said Ernie, all eyes now on him, and then, with theatrical timing, 'You were stood on the wall at the front conducting them!'

Cue the famous Moss grin, much to his amusement, but only I saw it, as everyone was looking astonished at me! Ah well, things turned out pretty

---

18 The Kop was a terraced area behind the goal at the Saltergate end of Chesterfield's old ground. See https://en.wikipedia.org/wiki/Spion_Kop_(stadiums)

well in the end, and the following season came the title.

I met Ernie coming out of Chesterfield College one evening, where he was doing a business studies course and I was studying for an Ordinary National Certificate in mechanical studies. He seemed a bit preoccupied so I asked if he was OK. He asked me how much I had earned the previous month, so I told him, £32. He then told me that because of contracted bonuses linked to wins and attendance sizes, etc., he had earned several times that amount, adding, 'That can't be right.'

I had to remind Ernie (at length!) that his job was by definition a relatively short employ, and that no one would begrudge him what he was earning. In any case, it was hardly a king's ransom.

I regard myself very fortunate to have called Ernie Moss a team-mate, a friend, and to have had him in my life as a footballing hero.

Without question he gave 100 per cent every time he pulled the shirt on, and he was so good that Chesterfield signed him three times over the years! My favourite goal of Ernie's? An overhead kick against Rotherham United away, made all the sweeter because it put paid to their undefeated home record in December 1970.

Crikey, don't I go on!

Gordon Harding was born 'over 70 years ago, a crowd's roar from Saltergate'. Trained as a draughtsman, he spent '40-odd years in the coal industry'. Gordon first saw Chesterfield play live in the 1955/56 season, a 1–0 defeat against Accrington Stanley in the old Third Division North, and describes himself as 'a Spireite till I die!' His love of Chesterfield is rivalled only by his devotion to his wife, Joyce, his two adult children, and his two grandchildren.

. . . .

Gordon goes on (some more)

Gordon Harding

'I just love talking about Ernie'

I've just been reminiscing about Ernie again, remembering his impish sense of humour.

I took my nephew to watch Chesterfield's reserve team playing a cup match. At half-time we changed ends by walking along the enclosure in front of the main Saltergate stand, and met Ernie near the players' entrance.

As we chatted, a number of the first-team players came out, and Ernie said, 'Come on, let's go and get a seat up in the stand.'

We were sitting as a group, taking up two rows, with my nephew very excited to be surrounded by his heroes! Then there suddenly appeared at the end of the row, a group of young autograph hunters, and autograph books were handed along from player to player. Each player signed and Ernie handed me the first of several books, nodding and telling me to sign my autograph, then pass it on, adding, 'They'll never know.'

After the game, as we were making our way to the exit, several young lads came up to me, passing Ernie, seeking my signature! (Mind you, I was sporting a fashionable leather bomber jacket and a Kevin Keegan hairstyle in those days.) I suggested they might not want my autograph, but they insisted. Ernie, standing watching, was near to bursting.

Looking at the scrawl on his page, one of the lads asked his mate, 'Who is it?' His friend said, 'I don't know but it will do for a swap!'

Years later I went in Moss & Miller to buy some football boots for my son, and Ernie introduced me to a visiting (very bemused) sales rep with the words, 'This is Gordon, he'll do for a swap!' Heaven knows what went through the poor man's head.

I just love talking about Ernie.

Kevin the kid meets his heroes

Kevin Oldfield

'A true gentleman and legend'

I grew up watching Ernie Moss and was always in awe of his heading ability. In particular, I remember watching him play and score a perfect hat-trick away at Walsall. Unfortunately, he still ended up on the losing side in that particular game, but it was a great goalscoring feat, all the same.

I started my football career in 1981 at Tube Investments Engineering Works in Chesterfield, which, unbeknown to me at the time, was the same place as Ernie began playing, some years earlier. I was then fortunate enough to be scouted, and in 1986 was invited to train with Chesterfield FC.

To say it was a dream come true is an understatement. I walked in to the dressing room on my first day and was instantly taken aback seeing all the pros sitting there, the very players I had idolised as a young fan at Saltergate.

To be honest, I was embarrassed to make eye contact with anyone, as I was some anonymous young kid in the presence of these giants, my footballing heroes.

Two players stood out immediately, but for opposite reasons. Chris 'Ged' Marples was loud and playful and Ernie Moss was silent and focused. Just before we left the changing rooms, Ernie spoke to me in a soft voice and was encouraging as he could tell I was nervous. Once we got down to the pitch on Piccadilly Road, Ernie was the first player to remove his tracksuit and start stretching and jogging round. Two hours later, as manager John Duncan told the first-team players to return to Saltergate, Ernie stopped back and did further shuttles, sprints, and shooting along with the trialists and apprentices.

He was still full of encouragement, stamina and enthusiasm even though he was in his twilight years in footballing terms, and the thing I remember was, he was the last to stop training. I was fortunate to remain on long-time trial through to the end of the season but sadly with no prior notice or knowledge Ernie left, along with Phil Brown, the following week. I was grateful for the opportunity to be on trial for so long and the greatest memory I have kept from those days was that of playing, training and meeting not only Kevin Randall, John Duncan, Dave Caldwell or even Jamie Hewitt but playing with the great Ernie Moss. Look up the meaning of a true gentleman and legend and it will say Ernie Moss.

Kevin Oldfield is a lifelong Spireite, growing up watching Chesterfield in the late 1970s and early '80s. Alan Birch and most of the 1980/81 team were his idols. Kevin started footballing at TI Chesterfield aged 16 and progressed to Chesterfield FC as a season-long trialist, playing 15 games in the reserves and scoring five goals. His favourite game was a reserve team cup match against Nottingham Forest, when John Duncan played ten first-team players alongside Kevin. Released from Chesterfield, he moved on to play for Staveley Miners Welfare and Borrowash Victoria, continuing to play Sunday league football into his 40s, despite breaking his back during one fixture. These days, Kevin and his dad are season ticket holders at Chesterfield, his father having been watching the club for something approaching 70 years. Kevin's son, now in his 30s, is continuing that family tradition, and has been the 'drummer boy' on the Kop for several seasons.

· · · ·

Sean and speeding

Sean O'Neill

'A great friend. Good memories'

Ernie loved to drive! So much so, he would never let me anywhere near the wheel whenever we were going places together. In fairness, he was a good driver and certainly liked to put his foot down. Woe betide anybody who overtook him!

For some reason best known to Ernie, he always drove with his fog lights on, even though for years I had been telling him that this was illegal. He simply took no notice.

One night we were on our way back from a game, somewhere over Lincoln way, I think, and as we were driving through the little villages a thick fog descended. As usual, Ernie was in a hurry to get home for his cup of tea but as we were navigating country roads, he couldn't really drive at the speeds he wanted to.

At one point, Ernie looked in his rear-view mirror and noticed a car coming up behind, which Ernie, unable to see properly because of the fog, thought was trying to overtake us. Not wanting to be outdone, he sped up a bit, gradually getting faster and faster until he realised the vehicle behind was in fact a police car.

When the patrol car reached us and overtook, they gradually slowed us down to about 30mph, even though Ernie still couldn't quite understand the need for such a drastic decrease in speed. That cuppa seemed a long way off!

This went on for a few miles, with us following the police, until the fog lifted as we were going through another village, at which point the blue lights were switched on and we were pulled over to the side of the road. The police officers in question took Ernie into their car and kept him there for about 20 minutes.

When he was allowed out, I asked him what had been going on and apparently their speed camera wasn't working so they couldn't actually book him for speeding, but they had caught him on another offence instead. Somewhat sheepishly, he confessed, 'They said the fog had lifted but I had committed the offence of driving while keeping my fog lights on.'

After all my words of warning over the years, all of which had been ignored, Ernie had finally been caught by the long arm of the law, and had to pay a fine. Enough said!

A great friend. Good memories.

Sean O'Neill was a versatile player who played almost 450 league games for Chesterfield and served as assistant manager to Ernie in non-league football once his own playing days were over. Belfast born, he filled six different positions in his first season (1974), and in 1985 received a Canon League loyalty award, enjoying a testimonial against Sheffield Wednesday. Sean retired from playing in 1986, with the fifth-highest number of league appearances for Chesterfield to his credit, and went on to coach junior sides at Rotherham United, Sheffield United and Doncaster Rovers, as well as coaching Chesterfield's under-16 team for a while.

. . . .

Asa's attempt

Asa Ingall

'You look like you were towing a caravan about out there!'

I'd been playing for Ernie and Sean O'Neill for a few seasons, but when I first arrived at Belper I was one of Ernie's early signings. Belper Town at that time, though, to be honest, weren't very good![19] We managed to stay up the first season and nearly made the play-offs the second season, but things never really panned out as we had hoped. Nevertheless, Ernie asked me to stay on for a third season as he remained convinced we would win promotion, but I'd only just got married and was concentrating

---

19 Ernie Moss was named manager of Northern Premier League team Belper Town in 2005. Belper finished 17th in 2004/05, but moved up to ninth in 2005/06, eight points off the play-offs. The Nailers dropped down to 19th in 2006/07, and Ernie parted ways with the club. Such is football!

on my new business and didn't think I could spare much time.

Ernie took the time to sit down with me and explained that I only had to make the games, and not to worry about training! On that basis, I signed, but we started the new season and things didn't go exactly to plan for the first few months. We were sitting frustratingly just outside the play-off places, but the team just wasn't clicking somehow, which was making Ernie and Sean very frustrated!

Juggling the demands of life as a newly married man and looking after my business, I somehow managed to pile on nearly three stone, so after the next game we played, which we should really have won quite easily but only drew, Ernie went mad in the changing rooms. He turned and looked at me and said, 'And you, you look like you were towing a caravan about out there! Slow and sluggish, how much weight have you put on?' I replied, 'Only a few pounds, Gaffer.' Well he went spare and stormed off into the physio rooms muttering something under his breath! The next thing, he comes out with some scales and places them in the middle of the changing rooms, telling me in no uncertain terms to get that claim checked. 'A few pounds! Get on them and let's see?'

I weighed at least 16 stone and of course everyone could tell, so I stood up, picked up the scales and moved them slightly while tampering with the little dial on top, so that they would make me appear lighter than I actually was.

The trouble was, though, I turned the dial a bit too far, which meant that according to Ernie's scales I'd suddenly lost five stone and was weighing in at 11 stone!

Some of the lads had seen what I'd done and burst out laughing. Eventually, everyone was laughing, apart from Ernie, that was. He made me run around the pitch 12 times, and I had to complete the feat in under 12 minutes, bearing in mind I'd just played for an hour and a half! My attempt at pulling a fast one on Ernie Moss didn't seem quite so funny after that, let me tell you!

Asa Ingall enjoyed a credible career in non-league football with numerous clubs, and was a popular player in and around the Derbyshire footballing circuit. When Ernie's daughter Sarah first read this story, before it went to print, she commented, 'Brilliant! No wonder Dad loved you!'

Phil's 48

Philip Marples

*'The only time I ever got to play sport
of any kind with Ernie Moss – he
ran me out!'*

The only time I ever met Ernie Moss was back in the late 1960s, somewhere around 1969, when we were both playing cricket for Staveley Chantry Youth Club at the Staveley ground, based at Middlecroft. At that time, I worked for East Midland Motor Services Ltd (now Stagecoach), and played cricket for the company, but on this occasion I was invited to turn out for Staveley against a team representing the General Post Office.

At the time I wasn't a batsman but a medium-pace bowler. However, on this particular occasion I had built up one of my best ever batting scores, having made 40-odd runs.

Then Ernie came in to bat!

After a little while, he tickled a ball down leg side and shouted 'Yes!' but by the time I had got away from my crease Ernie was at my end. It had only taken him what seemed like three strides to get there, his legs were that long!

Consequently I was run out, with my score at 48. Staveley Chantry went on to win the game, but I can't remember how many runs Ernie got that day.

My innings came to an end with me just short of my very first fifty. That was the only time I ever got to play sport of any kind with Ernie Moss, and he ran me out!

I am now nearer 80 than 70, but I will never forget that game of cricket, and neither will I forget Ernie Moss. I always wished him all the very best, even though I never did manage to repeat my batting score from that match.

So this is my one and only memory of the great Ernie Moss; a cricketing one, entirely unrelated to football!

He of course went on to play for Chesterfield and became nothing less than a legend.

Philip Marples used to go to watch Chesterfield play when they were in the old Fourth Division, although he never actually managed to ever see Ernie Moss in action. A fuel injection mechanic by trade, he has, at the time of writing, been married for almost 60 years. Sixty not out!

Memories from Mckay

Ian Mckay

'My first footballing hero'

Ernie, Ernie, Ernie, or Mossy was his name,
My first footballing hero,
Who gave everything for the game.
Standing on the Kop, swayed by the crowd,
Ernie, Ernie, Ernie,
We'd all shout your name out loud.

Ernie, Ernie, Ernie, you'd never let us down,
Floating like an eagle,
The talisman of the town.
You made scoring look so easy,
A tap-in or rocket shot,
But those fantastic bullet headers
Were the best goals of the lot.

Holmes passes to Randall,
Who works a magic trick:
Past the defender in a flash,
A quality cross to the back stick,
Rising like a giant,
From the genius he surely was,
Another quality goal from the legend, Ernie Moss.

So thanks for the memories,
The joy and pleasure you gave,
Ernie, Ernie, Ernie, there was never none so brave.
You're in Spireites' hearts for ever,
A legend to the core,
Ernie, Ernie, Ernie,
We'll sing your name forever more.

Ian Mckay, a resident of Chesterfield, submitted this poetic tribute along with the lovely statement, 'You're more than welcome to use it in the book or not – but I'll still buy your book.' A writer needs and appreciates contributors like that just as much as clubs like Chesterfield need and appreciate fans like Ian.

. . . .

David's diary

David Lilley

'He will always be remembered as a true club legend'

Always remembered. It began on 30 September 1980. It was a Tuesday night at Saltergate and represented my first-ever football match. Robert Lilley (my dad) had taken me along and we sat in the family stand, near the Kop end, on a cool autumn evening. As a 12-year-old, I was mesmerised by how green the pitch looked, illuminated by floodlights. The unique smell of Bovril and the chants of a home crowd, made up of over 6,600 scarf-clad fans, added to a wonderful atmosphere. I had never before been among so many people.

Colchester United were the opposition. Chesterfield started like a train and in the fourth minute, Ernie Moss scored!

The ground erupted with a deafening noise and the sort of gleeful celebrations to which I would become addicted, over the years. It all felt magical.

Phil Walker and Alan Birch (with a beautiful long-distance chip) scored second and third goals, in what was a scintillating first-half performance, the likes of which I have rarely seen since.

This was my first exposure to our reliable goal contributor Ernie Moss. It was my baptism to lower-league football and my love affair with the Spireites had begun.

Ernie went on to make more than 500 appearances and scored a club record 192 goals for Chesterfield.

I had the pleasure of meeting my hero during my Hallam FM days, when I interviewed him at the Moss

& Miller sports shop, ahead of a play-off final. When the club moved to the b2net stadium, Ernie would often chat to me and my wife, and would unfailingly smile at my babe-in-arms kids as we enjoyed the lounge hospitality before home games. I remember whispering to my wife (who is younger than me and not from Derbyshire), 'That's Ernie Moss. He is a true club legend!'

Today, whenever I think back and envision Chesterfield, the first picture I see is that of a tall Ernie Moss, wearing a blue-and-white-striped Coalite-sponsored shirt.

Likewise, when I think of the club's greatest ever servants, Ernie sits at the head of the honours list. He is a legend and an icon for me.

Ernie's service to Chesterfield FC and his passion to see the club succeed after his retirement means he earned an immortal presence in the hearts of true blues. He won a bond of unbreakable fondness and will always be remembered as a true club legend.

David Lilley is, quite simply, a Chesterfield fan, boy and man.

A smile for Sandra

Sandra Sharpe

'The most kind and loving man'

Working at Chesterfield Football Club, I got to meet a lot of footballers. I must say, Ernie was the most kind and loving man. He always had a smile for everyone.

Sandra Sharpe is a mother and grandmother, and worked as a hostess at Chesterfield FC for many years, meeting some very interesting people along the way.

. . . .

The man in black

Keith Hackett

'A great servant of the game'

I first met Ernie Moss early on in my refereeing career in the Football League. He was a tall, stand-out player who had this graceful leap whenever he rose to head the ball, which he did quite often!

As a referee, I particularly appreciated the fact that, with Ernie, there were no 'dark arts' of holding, pulling or going to ground at every opportunity; the sort of antics we now see all too often in so-called elite levels of the game. Ernie was honest and always afforded me great respect whenever our paths crossed on football fields here and there.

My memory of Ernie draws me to the occasional Sunday mornings when he would turn out for Derek Dooley's All-Star Eleven. Changing rooms were shared with everyone mucking in together, meaning that a plentiful supply of stories were exchanged. The likes of Johnny Quinn, Len Badger and Peter Swan would all have smiles on their faces as they put on their kits and tied up their boots.

Ernie would unfailingly respond to invitations to give of his services in charity games, and even in the face of enthusiastic opposition he would never lower his professional playing standards. That was quite typical of the man; giving of his best regardless of the stature or nature of the fixture, aware of his obligations to those who had come to see him play.

Ernie Moss rightly earned his status as a true legend of Chesterfield Football Club, although on those Sunday mornings he would also talk fondly of his time with Matlock Town, a club he had enjoyed being part of.

With that in mind, my hope is that the good people of Chesterfield and Matlock will now unite to erect a statue of Ernie in his honour.[20] He was indeed a great servant of the game.

Keith Hackett began refereeing in local leagues in the South Yorkshire area in 1960, and is counted among the top 100 referees of all time in a list maintained by the International Federation of Football History and Statistics. Graduating via the Northern Premier League and the Football League, he was senior linesman at the 1979 FA Cup Final and then referee at the 1981 final, the 100th FA Cup Final, at the age of just 36, subsequently being appointed to the prestigious FIFA list. Keith retired from top-flight refereeing just short of his 50th birthday in 1994. Among other activities in a busy retirement, he also contributes columns for the Sports Trader *magazine.*

Tim's tribute

Tim Fellows

*'On the team sheet, one name
… defines our hopes'*

Ernie
We all remember.

---

20 https://www.justgiving.com/campaign/ernie

The terraces, crumbling
under our frozen feet. Floodlights,
straining to light the four corners
of our hallowed field. Those minutes,
before gladiators appear, blue
scarves and hats streaming
in from Saltergate. Anticipation
rising like the steam
from the open roof of the toilet block.
Gloved hands, transferring
a 10p piece, receiving a programme
and some change. The metallic
clang, clang of the turnstile.

On the team sheet, one name,
one number, defines the team.
Lifts our hopes.

The local lad, plucked from his desk job,
leading from the front. The name,
chanted by the massed choir on the Kop,
his number, rising into the night sky,
propelled by willpower. That hanging
moment, when time stood still,
the crowd breathing in. We had been
in this moment before. Many times.

The head, meeting the ball, arcing
it towards the enfolding net. The roar,
straining the rusting roof, rattling
the ancient stand.

The noise fading in our minds,
into legend.

*Tim Fellows wrote this eloquent and evocative poem
in 2020. Tim started watching Chesterfield in 1965 at
the age of four, so his main years of supporting the club
'coincided with Ernie being the heart and soul of the team'.*

. . . .

Making his mark on Mark

Mark Kelly

'If you need any boots, let me know'

My friend Andy Baker told me a good story about
Ernie Moss.

Andy's nan and grandad, Jack and Martha
Steward, used to live in Hardwick Court, Staveley,
across the road from Ernie's mum, and one day Ernie
went over to talk to Andy when he saw some football
gear being loaded on to Andy's bike. He asked him

if he played and who he played for. When Andy said he played for Carr Vale, Ernie replied, 'Division One, you must be good. If you need any boots, let me know.'

Andy said Ernie knew his nan, his parents, and most of the people in the area.

Subsequently, Andy went to the Moss & Miller sports shop, and Ernie more or less gave him some boots for free, just wanting to encourage a young player. A few months later Ernie's mum came round and said, 'Ernie's sent these for your Andy. Size nine, isn't he.' Andy and Ernie got to know each other after that.

I think there are a few points in this little story that go to show what sort of man Ernie was, and why he was loved by so many people.

Incidentally, both Andy and I bought bricks to place in the newly erected Ernie Moss Wall of Fame. As it happens, I sent pictures of the bricks we had purchased to Ernie's daughter, Sarah, the day before he died. So very sad.[21]

Mark Kelly is just embarking on life in his 50s, while his friend and fellow Spireite Andy Baker is just a few years older. Mark has been a Chesterfield fan since 1981, having

---

21 Please see this link for details of the Ernie Moss Wall of Fame: https://chesterfield-fc.co.uk/commercial/ernie-moss-wall-of-fame

lived in the town all his life. Andy is a lifelong supporter,
originally from Bolsover but now living in Duckmanton
and attending matches with his daughter, Ruby.

. . . .

Duncan, Derby County and Duffield

John Duncan

'I have the greatest respect for
his football career'

The first time I saw Ernie play was when I attended an Anglo-Scottish Cup tie between Chesterfield and Glasgow Rangers, at Saltergate. I was at Derby County at the time and lived in Duffield, so my neighbour, John Jepson, who was an avid Chesterfield supporter, drove me to the match. I'd never been to Chesterfield before and John took me through the Amber Valley. It was stunning on a beautiful summer evening.

Ernie and his striking partner, Phil Walker (whom I subsequently re-signed for Chesterfield after he had been away from the club for a while), absolutely tore the Rangers defence to shreds. Ernie's movement was outstanding, holding play up and running into the channels. Chesterfield won 3-0 with Ernie, if my memory is right, scoring at least one of the goals.

My next contact with Ernie was once I became manager of Chesterfield in 1983. He was playing for Peterborough United at the time, I think, but also running Moss & Miller sports shop, which the club used for sports equipment and supplies.

At the end of the 1983/84 campaign we'd done reasonably well, but I felt we needed another striker if we wanted to be successful in the next season. Kevin Randall, who was part of our backroom staff in those days, had played with Ernie and knew him well. As we knew Ernie was available, he became part of our discussions. I said that I liked him but I needed someone who, apart from having a good goals record, would have to have a 'good engine' too, in order to cover right across and up and down the

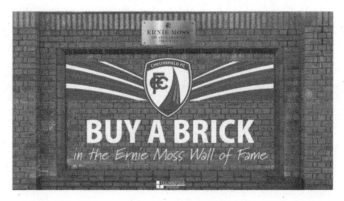

field, into both channels, and that I honestly thought Ernie's age went against him in terms of being able to do that. Kevin reassured me that I didn't need to have any worries about Ernie's fitness. He told me that Ernie would be the fittest player at the club and would train hard every day. Kevin was confident that Ernie would be as strong in the 90th minute as he was in the first.

Trusting Kevin's advice, I got on the phone immediately, and we signed Ernie the next day. He turned out to be one of my best signings as a manager. In my view, he was one of the best headers of a football in the world. His heading was invaluable at both ends of the pitch; scoring at one end, for example, but also, as I vividly remember on more than one occasion, heading clear late on in matches when we were protecting a slender lead. He was also a very good first-time finisher with his feet, having the ability to adjust his footwork and hit the target, however the ball came to him.

I particularly recall a game at Halifax when Ernie was just two goals short of achieving a prestigious scoring landmark, either 100 goals for Chesterfield or 200 goals in his career. I think he scored in the first half and we were awarded a penalty which might well have completed the feat. I waved for him to come over to the dugout where I said, 'You take the penalty.' He replied, 'I've scored 99 goals so far without taking a penalty and I don't want to start now.' Bob Newton scored from the spot and Ernie got another late on, so everyone was pleased.

Ernie wanted to play in every single game but towards the end of the season I felt playing Ernie at home, where we were likely to get crosses in and make chances, was essential. Away from home, however, I preferred Phil Walker up front, as he was effective on the break and was able to play wide as a creator rather than a scorer. Bob Newton had a great season, was top scorer and was a fixture as a partner to either Ernie or Phil.

I didn't think it right to tell Phil and Ernie my away/home strategy, with Ernie being naturally upset when he was left out. However, to his credit he came to me and said, 'I don't like this in and out situation but I understand why you are doing it.'

That incident, and the Halifax penalty story, summed up so much of his attitude to teamwork. Ernie was great to manage, being self-motivated, and understanding some of the decisions that a manager has to make. He was the ultimate professional. We went on to win the championship in 1985, which we wouldn't have done without Ernie.

In the close-season I signed Dave Caldwell, a pacy goalscorer I thought would gel with Ernie. Unfortunately, though, as sometimes happens in football, that partnership didn't quite work and I therefore allowed Ernie to move to Stockport County. I subsequently went to see County play, and I remember Ernie being outstanding. I also remember driving home after that game thinking I'd made a big mistake in letting him go!

To be honest, I didn't know Ernie well enough to have a big personal relationship with him but Kevin Randall fitted that role excellently and only ever spoke highly of him as a friend and a colleague. Latterly, I saw Ernie regularly at home games in the new stadium and at events such as reunion dinners. I have the greatest respect for his football career and feel privileged to have worked with and known him.

As we all know, Ernie had very difficult health issues to contend with during the last years of his life. The way he and his family faced up to them, though, is a credit to them all.

John Duncan was a popular forward who played for Dundee, Tottenham Hotspur, Derby County and Scunthorpe United. He also represented the Scottish Football League. During his four years at Spurs, Duncan averaged more than one goal every two games: 53 goals in 103 appearances, with a very respectable career total of 129 goals in 269 league matches. He went on to manage Scunthorpe United, Hartlepool United, Ipswich Town, Chesterfield (twice) and Loughborough University, leading Chesterfield to Third Division play-off glory in 1995 and, famously, the FA Cup semi-final in 1997, only losing to Middlesbrough in controversial circumstances – an infamous defeat that still rankles among Chesterfield fans. Sadly, John passed away in October 2022. This piece, therefore, is included not only in memory of Ernie Moss, but of John too, a real 'footballing man' who was held in high regard throughout the game.

. . . .

Carol considered it a privilege

Carol Neale

'Rest in peace, my good friend'

I've known Ernie since I was a little girl, as my dad and Ernie's dad worked together.

As the years went on Ernie Moss became my Spireites hero. I have been privileged to be a part of Team Ernie and helped with fundraising for research into dementia.

Ernie's family have been kind enough to include me in his birthday celebrations over the years, and because of this I feel humbled and honoured to have known such a kind and gentle man.

His love for his family and friends was unconditional.

Rest in peace, my good friend.

Carol Neale was born in Chesterfield in 1955. Her father worked at Staveley Works and Tube Works, while her mother worked at Robinsons in the town. Marrying in 1976, she now has two grown-up children and two 'adorable grandsons'. A few years ago, Carol worked with Ernie's daughter Nikki at a local primary school, and was able to reconnect with the Moss family.

. . . .

Siddon's soliloquy

Chris Siddon

As we say goodbye to a true club legend, I thought I'd
   post my feeble efforts at poetry again.
No other player has stirred such emotions in me to
   the extent that I would actually share my thoughts,
   but this is for Ernie.
God bless our Ernie and his truly wonderful family.

Son of Chesterfield,

Son of the spire,

No one ever questioned his desire.

A true gentleman on the field and off

A legend who deserves to be carried high and aloft.

He'd even show us what trainers or what cricket
    whites to buy;

No air or graces you'd see in his shop,

All the time in the world he would share

To make sure your footie boots were the right pair.

No bling, no chav, he was just another Chesterfield lad,

But us Spireites know that's not true:

Cut our Ernie and he'd bleed blue.

If he was a stick of rock it would read 'Spireite'.

Not old enough to see him play first time around,

You could tell that Saltergate was his special ground,

His testimonial richly deserved no 'go away' would
    be heard

As Spireites queued up for him to sign. I still have
    that programme that he signed.

Called 'Big Ernie' for more than just his stature

As he went about creating another Chesterfield
    chapter,

A chapter that had it all from all the record-breaking
    goals he'd score, two titles,

A cup as well, a hometown boy so proud

The fans chanted 'Ernie, Ernie, Ernie' really loud.

What honours can we bestow?

A road, what next, a statue? I might suggest, paid for by the fans that should be the way, Ernie pointing us back to a better day.

Going down Ernie Moss Way makes a Spireite feel proud

All I want to do is shout 'Ernie, Ernie, Ernie' out loud.

What wouldn't we do to have a player of his stature now,

And sing 'He's one of our own, he's one of our own'.

Ernie Moss will always be one of our own.

We all know he was born under the shadow of our spire

And nobody in the world could ever question his desire.

So when you see a player who doesn't give a toss

Just think 'you're not fit to lace the boots of our Ernie Moss'.

Chris Siddon first penned these words on Facebook's Chesterfield FC Fans Group page, shortly after Ernie Moss died. They were posted on Facebook to coincide with Ernie's funeral.[22]

---

22 https://www.facebook.com/groups/482781205134474

Everlasting love

Taking after Grandad – Fin and Callie

Supporting Chesterfield FC at Stamford Bridge 2022

Celebrating Ernie's 70th birthday

Matchday – Ernie's 70th

Preparing for charity match with Fin, Callie and Erin

With Nikki and Stu

Thoughtful moment with Sarah and Georgia

Ernie enjoying the day

Standing ovation

Ernie, Nikki and Georgia

Ernie with Georgia, Fin and Callie

Memorable day with Jenny and Sarah

Unveiling Ernie's mosaic with family

Presenting the match ball – Ernie Moss Day 2017

Hollingworth's hero

Glyn Hollingworth

'One of our town's greats'

Everyone from Chesterfield knew Ernie. In the '80s he was my hero, when I was only 14 years old.

My biggest memory of him wasn't one from Saltergate, but going into his sports shop, Moss & Miller. My friends and I would walk down to Brampton and if we spotted him in there we couldn't resist but go inside to say hello to Ernie.

At that age, we never had any money, really, but Ernie didn't seem to care about that. He was never going to be a Mike Ashley! We would stand and chat football for hours on end with him and he always gave us his time, talking headers – and Bob Newton misses! Ernie's shop became a hub for folk that not only wanted sports gear but also wanted to feel a connection to one of our town's greats.

Ernie Moss was one of the nicest men I have ever met in my life. Chesterfield lost a great guy when he left us. He was one of ours.

Our Ernie. He was a credit to our town, and he leaves behind a wonderful family.

God bless, my mate x

Glyn Hollingworth and his friends Ricky Corillo, Andrew Dudley and Mick Dawes were all Brampton lads. Glyn lived on Chester Street with his mum and dad, Don and Maureen, very close to the Moss & Miller shop. Don Hollingworth was a fruit and veg merchant on Chesterfield market and knew Ernie very well. He also knew Geoff Miller, Ernie's great friend and business partner.

. . . .

David's deal of the decade

David McPhie

'The glory that was an Ernie Moss goal'

No, Ernie didn't play for England. Nor did he set the First Division alight. His career was spent, and his 245 league goals were scored (162 for Chesterfield) primarily in the Third and Fourth Divisions.

I happen to believe, though, that, had some enterprising manager taken a chance on him, Ernie Moss could have prospered as a goalscorer at a club in the lower reaches of the (then) First Division, or maybe the upper half of the old Second Division. I think he was that good.

I contend that such a move, particularly if it had been in tandem with his 'partner in crime' Kevin

Randall, would have resulted in one of the bargain buys of the decade.

Such a bold move in the transfer market was not without precedent, as in the 1970s Ted McDougall and Phil Boyer formed an extremely prolific strike partnership in the lower leagues for York City and Bournemouth, before moving up the 'league ladder' to prosper in the First Division with both Norwich City and Southampton.

The Kevin and Ernie partnership, forever to be cherished in Saltergate folklore, has lived on, undimmed, in the memories and affections of those of us lucky enough to have been regular attendees during that successful late 1960s/early 1970s era. However, now that so many of us are passing on it is perhaps timely to remind those who are too young to have seen the glory that was an Ernie Moss goal, that his contribution to the history and spirit of this proud club should be forever enshrined in a special place in its history.

Ernie's family have much to be proud of in the life of such a Chesterfield footballing legend and local cultural hero.

David McPhie was born in 1941, and was a regular Chesterfield supporter through the 1950s to the 1970s, returning a few seasons ago. He has the distinction of having been a drummer with the 1960s group the Blueberries, and was involved in helping none other than Joe Cocker secure a recording contract. David now runs the High Peak Bookstore & Café (www.highpeakbookstore. co.uk) in Buxton.

. . . .

The chaplain chips in

Paul Hollingworth

'The example to us all was that a hero operates both on and off the pitch'

Having lived and worked in Chesterfield all my life, a walk up Chatsworth Road was nothing out of the ordinary. One wintry morning I was stopped by a polite gentleman sweeping the front of the old GK Ford site. The excitement at bumping into someone I knew as a childhood hero was still very real, yet still he made time to chat with me about memories from the '80s.

Ernie Moss was more than just a memory of the good old days; he was a true gentleman. This was the same man who brought so much hope to so many people, even on cold, dark, Saltergate Tuesday nights. There was something magical about the fact that even on a dark, dreary evening, Ernie could bring a glimmer of hope, a corner, a flick-on, just maybe something could happen.

I guess through life we meet many fascinating people but not everyone has that ability to cause you to stand on your tiptoes and peer over the heads in front of you, in anticipation that something was going to happen. It was only a corner and we have not come close to scoring all night but this could be it. Ernie is in the box and jostling to get his head on any potential opportunity that came his way to bring a sense of happiness to a few thousand people. Sometimes making people's dreams come true requires someone to put themselves in a position of discomfort to bring about great joy for the others. This was the Ernie that we all knew.

Then to find myself face to face with this legendary man was where I discovered what real heroes are like. 'Good morning, young man,' said the hero stooped over with a broom in his hand, breathing in the cold winter air. It was not the most ideal moment for a conversation but that says a lot about the man.

Not only was Ernie Moss able to captivate many people's attention while he played on his stage but he had the same aura off the stage. The example to us all was that a hero operates both on and off the pitch. He showed it was possible to play both roles and do it well. If only we could all learn a little something from his life and bring some hope and joy to all the people we meet.

Pastor Paul Hollingworth, of the Lifehouse Church in Chatsworth Road (www.lifehousechurch.co.uk), Chesterfield, is chaplain to Chesterfield Football Club.

. . . .

Gareth and the Gladiators

Gareth Davis

'An excellent footballer and an even better human being'

Working on this book has been a very enjoyable experience, both from a professional perspective as a copy editor and also on a personal level as a football fan, reading so many great and heartfelt stories about Ernie Moss.

Through communicating with Stephen I have shared a few of my own personal memories of Ernie, and I was touched when he asked me to put together this contribution. I was delighted to do so.

I must have been ten or 11 when Ernie signed for Matlock Town in the early 1990s, too young to have seen him play professionally, although my dad knew all about his career and put me in the picture. I was excited that someone of Ernie's standing had joined the Gladiators.

Confession time – I remember very little about Ernie's spell in a Matlock shirt, although it has been interesting to read other people's recollections of his playing style, particularly his overhead kicks. Because – and this is genuine, no journalistic licence here – when I think of Ernie playing for Matlock, my only recollection is of him attempting an overhead kick!

Moss & Miller in Matlock was a regular stop for me to get some new boots or goalkeeping gloves, and fast forward to 2001, Ernie was appointed as manager at Causeway Lane, by which time I was the sports editor of the *Matlock Mercury*, the local newspaper, and also the club's stadium announcer.

I could never claim to have known Ernie well on a personal level but we spoke a lot professionally over the three years he was in charge, and he was never anything other than polite, courteous, and happy to talk to me.

Ernie would always take the time out of his schedule every week to go over all things Matlock

Town during a period in which he took over the club after a rocky couple of seasons and stabilised things, introduced some quality players, and led the Gladiators to finish second in the table and a first trophy in 12 years during his final season.

And, just for good measure, I've also played alongside Ernie!

That was in the spring of 2005 and a fundraising match at Matlock for the club's new stand appeal, a cause Ernie had always been fully supportive of and involved with during his time in the Causeway Lane dugout.

It was a Matlock Town fans and legends XI against a Derby County legends XI, and as a lifelong supporter of both it was a wonderful experience for me personally.

I say 'alongside' – I was in goal and Ernie was, of course, leading the line in attack.

A decade or so later came another fundraising game at Matlock, although this time in Ernie's honour, after his condition had been diagnosed.

It involved former players from Matlock and also Belper Town, our local – but friendly – rivals, where Ernie finished his managerial career, and more than £1,000 was raised on a day which attracted a very healthy crowd.

The day also showed just how highly Ernie is thought of by friends, colleagues, former players and football fans alike; so many people turned up from all facets of his life to support him and such a worthy cause. The football family indeed.

Typical of the man, he made time to say hello to everyone who wanted to pass on their best wishes. And there were a lot of people who wanted to see him.

The annual pre-season friendly between Matlock and Chesterfield is now played for the Ernie Moss Challenge Cup, a fitting tribute to a man with such deep links to both clubs.

I'll hand over now to the most important people in Ernie's life, who will complete the story of someone who was an excellent footballer and an even better human being.

Gareth Davis is a Matlock Town and Derby County supporter of more than 30 years' standing, and an occasional visitor to Chesterfield. He was a sports journalist and latterly a matchday programme editor, and as well as being a published author he also now operates as a copy editor and proofreader (https://gtn.media/). Gareth has worked with the publishers, Pitch Publishing, on Ernie!. *This is the 399th book edit of his career!*

One of their own

Chesterfield Football Club

Following the sudden and unexpected passing away of Ernie Moss in July 2021, senior club officials at Ernie's beloved Chesterfield FC paid tribute to a true Spireites legend.

These words of tribute and remembrance go some way towards expressing the esteem, respect and affection in which Ernie was held. They are shared here courtesy of the club's official Facebook page:

Chief executive John Croot: One of the highlights for me when I was a young lad following Chesterfield was watching Ernie play. You knew when you saw his name on the team sheet that there was a good chance he would score.

Ernie would give his all for Chesterfield and that made him a very popular figure with supporters. His dedication and professionalism shone through and he will always feature when people from that era talk about their favourite players.

Chairman Mike Goodwin: I remember standing on the Kop, chanting 'Ernie, Ernie, Ernie!' Ernie was an old-fashioned centre-forward who led the line well. He was a great goalscorer.

Later, after Ernie had ended his playing career, I used to visit the Moss & Miller sports shop and chat to Ernie. It's a sad loss to lose someone of Ernie's standing.

Commercial manager and former team-mate Jim Brown: I was really sad to hear the news about Ernie, a local lad who became a legend for his hometown club.

He was a player who always gave 100 per cent effort at all times and he was a joy to play alongside, someone you could always rely on as a friend and team-mate.

The number of goals he scored and the appearances he made speak volumes for the man he was. When you heard the fans shout 'Ernie, Ernie, Ernie!' the opposition team knew they were in for a difficult day.

He will be greatly missed by his friends and footballing colleagues and our thoughts are with Ernie's wife Jenny and his family at such a sad time.

. . . .

Goodbye to a goalscoring great

The following paragraph was published in the *Derbyshire Times* dated Tuesday, 3 August 2021, giving details of Ernie's funeral service, which took place at Chesterfield Crematorium on Friday, 6 August 2021:

'Much-loved Ernie, Chesterfield's all-time record goalscorer, passed away aged 71 last month after battling dementia. Funeral directors Harold Lilleker & Sons Ltd said on Tuesday, "On Friday Ernie will be making his final journey to the celebration of his life.

'"We will leave from our Whittington Moor funeral home on Friday at 2.10pm. Ernie's family and friends will be collected, then we will pass the former Saltergate ground as we travel back to the Technique Stadium. Supporters and friends are invited to gather outside the Technique Stadium by 2.50pm where we will take him on a lap of honour and say goodbye with a minute's applause at 3pm. As we leave the stadium Ernie will travel along Ernie Moss Way to Chesterfield Crematorium for his service at 3.10pm. Outside speakers will be on for those wishing to stand outside the service."'[23]

---

23 Reproduced by kind permission of Phil Bramley, editor of the *Derbyshire Times*.

Ernie's funeral service attracted interest from countless newspapers and media outlets, and was reported on by television channels. After the funeral procession passed Ernie's old haunt at Saltergate, the service was held at a packed Chesterfield Crematorium. With many more listening outside, Ernie was described as 'a gentleman in everything he did'.

Harold Lilleker & Sons Ltd, who looked after Ernie in the days directly before his final farewell, have not only sent their good wishes for the success of this book, but have also contributed the following comment.

'It was a wonderful service and I noticed the other day our video of the minute's applause on Facebook has been watched 6.7 million times.'[24]

Six point seven million times! Says it all, really.

. . . .

---

24 By kind permission of Drew Lilleker.

A family funeral

One of the tributes shared at Ernie's funeral service
Kind courtesy of Sarah Moss

'Love you forever'

As a family we would like to thank you all for joining us in celebrating Ernie's life.

To say we will miss you beyond measure is an understatement.

The hole you leave behind can never be filled, but we will always remember you with love and joy, like you would want us to, not sadness.

Your were the best husband/dad/grandad to us all, you always put us first and everything you did in life was for us.

We will keep doing our best to make you proud and hope you are watching over us, protecting and guiding us, like you did in life.

We want to thank you for making us the people we are today and for showing us what true love is.

Night, God bless.

Until we meet again.

Love you forever

xx

Georgia's grandad

Georgia Trueman

'To have called this legend my grandad is an absolute honour'

For as long as I can remember, my grandad was always my biggest inspiration.

Growing up, I never really understood why everyone called him a legend, as I just knew him as Grandad, an honest, caring and loving man who always put his family first.

This in itself was enough for him to be a role model to all his grandchildren; someone we always looked up to and loved spending time with.

As I grew older, I loved hearing about his playing days and watching recordings of some of his media interviews. Grandad's passion for football shone through his words.

Even when my wonderful grandad became ill, he still loved watching Chesterfield play. He adored that club!

The pure dedication Ernie Moss had for his beloved sport, along with the unconditional love and support I received from him, has encouraged me to follow all my dreams as an athlete and as a person.

I can speak for all the family when I say his smile, laugh and hugs warmed us up inside, reminding us, even when he was ill, of the funny, kind-hearted person he always was.

To have been able to call this legend my grandad is an absolute honour, and all our memories of him will now be cherished forever.

Georgia Trueman is the daughter of Ernie's daughter, Nikki.

. . . .

Callie counts her memories

Callie Moss

'I love and miss you so much'

Grandad, I remember coming to see you and Nanna every day and playing football, or catch, in the garden.

I remember when we took you to watch Chesterfield, we would go in the lounge and I would always make you a cup of tea.

I remember coming to see you in the nursing home, and feeding you your dinner, playing cards and looking at football books. They were good times.

I remember the last time I saw you. At the time I didn't realise it would be the last time, but now that moment will forever stick in my memory.

I love and miss you so much, and would do or give anything in this world to have you back, or see you one more time.

Grandad, I love you with all my heart and I always will, no matter what.

Grandad, you will be missed forever, but never forgotten.

Love forever,

Callie xxxxxxx

Callie Moss is the daughter of Ernie's daughter, Sarah.

· · · ·

Finlay's fond farewell

Finlay Moss

'The last time I saw you ... will remain one of the greatest days of my life'

Grandad, I remember taking you to Chesterfield games and singing to the chants with you, and you used to tap people's heads on the row in front, with your programme or gloves.

I remember coming to see you in the summer and playing football in the garden in the sun.

I remember coming to visit you in the nursing home, and feeding you cheese on toast or a Sunday dinner.

In lockdown we came to see you through the window and hold your hand, as that's all we were allowed to do.

I remember the time we went out for Nanna's birthday, and we brought you along as a surprise for her. Nanna loved it and we had a lovely meal.

I remember the last time I saw you, and that will remain one of the greatest days of my life.

Grandad, I love and miss you so much, and I would give anything in the world to see you again, one last time.

Grandad, I love you and I always will.

Love forever,

Fin

xxxxxxxx

Finlay is Sarah Moss's son.

. . . .

The man who made so many Moss memories

Firstly, as a family we would like to thank Stephen for producing this book, an everlasting tribute to Dad. It's taken him a lot of time, dedication, love and commitment. We can't ever thank him enough. Secondly, we want to thank everyone who has contributed their own personal stories and memories of Dad, whether that be on a footballing or on a personal level. Michael South has provided so many excellent photographs, and we are more than grateful to him for his help and cooperation. Accompanied by Michael's photography, these memories are lovely to read and just prove what a gentleman Dad was, and how he made a huge impact on and off the field.

When we first started working on this book, Dad was still alive, but living in care, ravaged by the vile disease that is dementia. It's been a long, cruel journey that eventually stripped Dad of his empathy, speech, social skills, memory and dignity. Sadly on Sunday, 11 July 2021, after fighting a battle he was never going to win, Dad took his last breath and closed his eyes forever. That day was the worst day of our lives, but he was finally at peace.

Upon his death, we as a family made the heartbreaking decision to donate his brain for the ongoing research being carried out by Dr Willie Stewart, the neuropathologist at the Queen Elizabeth Hospital in Glasgow. During a lockdown Zoom call, Dr Stewart gave us the news which we deep down already knew:

Dad had high levels of Chronic Traumatic Encephalopathy (CTE) in his brain, caused by repeated head trauma. Football was Dad's life, so it's devastating to think it also contributed to his death. However, despite the sadness and irony of that tragedy, we don't want to focus on all the bad bits, and this book is a special way of remembering Dad and celebrating his life.

As a family, we have millions of happy memories. Our main footballing ones are of Saltergate; happy days watching from the wooden stands as Dad played, week in and week out. He would always look up and wave to us when he scored, and we were the proudest girls in the world.

Dad had time for literally everyone he met, and was so humble, never turning down a request for an autograph or photo to be taken, even though he never really understood why, which speaks volumes for his natural modesty. In his eyes, he was a normal bloke, simply doing a job he loved to the best of his ability, but to the rest of us he was a LEGEND.

Away from football, Dad was a true family man, devoted husband, dad and grandad, which was probably a side of his life and personality not many people got to see; family holidays abroad every summer, the long walks with our dog, the singing along to Meat Loaf and the Hollies, the laughter and love. It was Dad and his girls against the world! Dad taught us so much in life; to be kind, have manners, to be respectful, to believe in ourselves, and how to love. Consequently, he now lives on in the beautiful grandchildren he loved so dearly, and they will do him proud and carry on his legacy.

And lastly – thank you, Dad, for every single thing you ever did for us, for never doubting us, and for loving us more than life itself. Night, God bless, until we meet again.

Love you forever,

Jenny, Sarah and Nikki xxxxxxxx

. . . .

Michael's memories

Michael South

'It has been an honour and an absolute pleasure to have photographed him'

Rest in peace, Ernie Moss.

Ernie was a born-and-bred Chesterfield gentleman who went on to become a Chesterfield FC legend. He played for and managed many teams during his 39-year footballing career, but he was best known for scoring 192 Spireite goals, which remains an unbeaten club record for his hometown club.

Ernie's natural skill as a goalscorer, though, came at a price, as in 2014 he was diagnosed with a rare form of frontotemporal dementia which his family, having received expert medical advice, believe came from years of heading the heavy old-school leather footballs.

Since Ernie's diagnosis there have been many charity football games and events held to help raise awareness and funds aimed at finding a cure for this horrible disease.

As a professional photographer, but more so as a CFC fan, I first became involved with the Moss family back in 2016, photographing Ernie's Once

Upon a Smile charity football game. To be honest, it has been an honour and an absolute pleasure to have photographed him.

So, who was Ernie Moss?

First and foremost he was a proud family man. In addition to that he was a phenomenal footballer with skill and integrity, but then if you are from Chesterfield, you will already have known that. Allow me to introduce you to him.

Ernest Moss was born on 19 October 1949 in Hollingwood, Chesterfield. From an early age he showed a raw talent with a ball, so much so that at the age of 17 he was signed by Chesterfield, from his local Tube Works team. Ernie's position was always up front as a striker, which is where he started the first of his 17 games that season, making his debut against Bradford in October 1968. In his first year, Ernie helped the Spireites go on to win the Northern Intermediate League Cup, so he clearly made an immediate impact.

This was the first of three spells at Chesterfield over a long career that spanned three decades. His original spell at the club was the longest, lasting seven years from 1968 to 1975, during which Ernie played 271 league games, scoring an impressive 95 goals, many with his head.

During his time at Saltergate, Chesterfield's home ground, Ernie married Jenny in 1971, and they went on to have two daughters, Nikki and Sarah.

After a few seasons away from Chesterfield playing for Peterborough United and Mansfield Town, Ernie returned to Saltergate in 1979, his goals helping Chesterfield to secure the 1981 Anglo-Scottish Cup and nearly winning promotion too. Sadly, though, due to a pay dispute, Ernie rejected the offer of a new contract and decided to leave the club in order to play his football for Port Vale in the June of 1981.

Fast forward five years, during which time Ernie also played for Lincoln City and Doncaster Rovers, to when Chesterfield's then manager, John Duncan, brought him back to Saltergate for a third and final time. Chesterfield went on to win the 1984/85 Fourth Division title. Ernie's goals, many of which were headers, helped the club achieve promotion, but his skill at being a prolific header of the ball would so tragically come back to haunt him and his family.

Ernie was subsequently transferred to Stockport County, where he played one season before moving on to sign for Scarborough. The last two of Ernie's professional career goals were scored while he was out on loan at Rochdale, after which he decided to retire from full-time football.

An interesting light-hearted fact to mention here is that of all his 240-plus goals, Ernie Moss never scored one from the penalty spot. He nearly did, though, as in his 1986 Chesterfield v Sheffield United testimonial game, he took his first and only penalty – but missed!

In summary, during his three spells at the club, Ernie made a total of 539 appearances for the Spireites, scoring a record 192 goals in the process – a terrific achievement.

Ernie's next step was into the world of football management, which is where he stayed for the next 15 years, employed as an assistant and first team manager with Boston United, Gainsborough Trinity (where he had two spells), Leek Town, Kettering Town, Matlock Town, Hucknall Town and Belper Town. During his time in the dugout Ernie won some silverware, namely the Northern Premier League Challenge Cup and the Peter Swales Shield with Gainsborough (both in 1997), and the Derbyshire Senior Cup with Matlock Town in 2004. Ernie ended his managerial days at Belper Town in 2007.

Throughout his footballing days Ernie was also a successful businessman, as co-owner of the sports shop Moss & Miller, in partnership with the Derbyshire and England cricketer Geoff Miller. Together they ran two shops, located in Chesterfield and Matlock. Over the years, though, Ernie was forced to slow down his pace in life, resulting in a formal diagnosis of dementia, the dreadful news being imparted to Ernie and his family in 2014.

In retirement, Ernie was always a regular at home games of his beloved Chesterfield FC, attending with his family. With the wholehearted support of the club, they began to organise fundraising matches in support of dementia charities.

With Ernie's diagnosis confirmed, and dementia slowly beginning to take its toll, Chesterfield FC designated their home games against Port Vale in 2015 and 2016 as Ernie Moss Day. All monies raised with various fundraising initiatives were donated to his chosen dementia charities.

A further acknowledgement of Ernie's status within the town came in 2017, when Chesterfield Borough Council elected to re-name the road next to Chesterfield's stadium Ernie Moss Way.

Ernie attended his final home game on his 70th birthday in 2019. I met up with him and his family in the club bar, prior to the match, to take a few photos. It was breathtaking to hear the fans all cheering for him at the 70th minute of play! Shortly after this, due to his dementia, his family made the heartbreaking decision to move Ernie into a nursing home that would better meet his care needs. Sadly, Ernie passed away there in 2021.

It's a crying shame that the sport Ernie loved inadvertently robbed him of his later years with his family. There is one thing, though, that cannot be taken away and that is his fantastic footballing legacy. Ernie is still well loved by all who have met and worked with him. The fans still talk about him and that's what will live forever; that and photographs of him scoring his amazing goals.

In the reception area at Chesterfield Football Club there is a mosaic showing Ernie heading the ball into the net, in characteristic style. That tribute is of course a bittersweet memory nowadays, but it has its rightful place there. It will stand proud for many a year, showcasing Chesterfield's greatest ever goalscorer. You can be sure of that!

Michael South is a Chesterfield-based photographer offering all types of photographic services, from local landscape canvases such as the famous Crooked Spire and Bolsover Castle to weddings, christenings and family portrait photography. Being a Derbyshire local, he also photographs games and events at Chesterfield and Matlock Town, and produces his own monthly Spireite page for two

magazines. *Supporting Chesterfield, he was privileged to have worked with the Moss family for Ernie's charity football games and social events at the club, from 2016 to 2019. To see further photography of Ernie Moss, check out Michael's website at michaelsouthphotography.com.*

· · · ·

The Ernie Moss Memorial Campaign

An appeal has been launched, by the Chesterfield FC Community Trust (http://spireitestrust.org.uk/), with the hope and intention of raising funds so that a permanent memorial to Ernie can be placed in the Chesterfield FC Memorial Garden. A portion of the royalties from sales of this book will be donated to the campaign.

You are warmly invited to read that story below and consider making a donation. Even better, if you feel able to organise a special fundraising event, then please make contact with the Community Trust and let them know what you have in mind. Ideas welcome! Contact details are listed below, so please feel free to get in touch.

Spireites legend Ernie Moss, Chesterfield's record goalscorer and undoubtedly one of the town's greatest sons, fully deserves a permanent memorial of some kind. Ernie has a road named after him, but the trustees and friends of the memorial garden feel a memorial would be a fitting tribute to a great man who gave so much to the town and to the club.

To that end, a fundraising campaign is under way, hoping to raise £71,000 in respect of the fact that Ernie passed away at the age of 71.

All donations, large or small, will be gratefully received, whether these are from individuals or from businesses or sports clubs wishing to help commemorate a local hero.

A permanent memorial will remind fans of Chesterfield Football Club, as well as fans of visiting teams, just what Ernie meant to so many people.

In respect of Ernie's status as a legendary number eight, donations featuring the number eight are especially welcome!

Please follow this link and let's see if together, we can make this happen: https://www.justgiving.com/campaign/ernie.

On behalf of Ernie's family, and some of the team heading up the appeal, Peter Whiteley, Paul Goodwin, Alan Wilkinson, Ian Browes, John Croot, Nick Johnson, Terry Ward, Paul Kellett, Stuart Basson, Keith Jackson and Phil Tooley, thank you.

Moss and a magpie

Alan Shearer

Former England international Alan Shearer investigated the potentially devastating link between football and dementia in a one-hour documentary that was broadcast by the BBC in 2017.[25]

Scientific reports from around the world have revealed that the link between football and dementia could be a result of brain damage caused by heading

---

25 *Alan Shearer: Dementia, Football and Me.*

the ball. At the time of writing, Alan remains the Premier League's all-time top scorer with a remarkable 260 goals, 46 of which were scored with headers.

With reports of a worrying number of the legendary England 1966 team suffering from dementia, the Newcastle United legend has a vested interest regarding football's potential links with brain injury.

Approached to comment on this situation, Alan stressed the need for further research, and kindly offered these words for inclusion in this book, 'Research has shown that former professional footballers are three and a half times more likely to die of dementia than people of the same age range in the general population. We've all seen the devastating impact this illness has, not just on the people it attacks but their friends and family as well. I sincerely hope that football can learn from the lessons of the past to protect the players of the future.'

. . . .

The final whistle

The man himself

'For me, competing was all about the pride and dignity of honest endeavour, and winning wasn't all about riches and rewards, it was about preserving one's sporting integrity, it was about honour.'[26]

---

26 https://en.wikipedia.org/wiki/Ernie_Moss